Martin Gassel

Influence of Noise, Variability, and Time-Delayed Feedback on Networks

Martin Gassel

Influence of Noise, Variability, and Time-Delayed Feedback on Networks

Dynamics of Neural Networks

Südwestdeutscher Verlag für Hochschulschriften

Impressum/Imprint (nur für Deutschland/ only for Germany)
Bibliografische Information der Deutschen Nationalbibliothek: Die Deutsche Nationalbibliothek verzeichnet diese Publikation in der Deutschen Nationalbibliografie; detaillierte bibliografische Daten sind im Internet über http://dnb.d-nb.de abrufbar.
Alle in diesem Buch genannten Marken und Produktnamen unterliegen warenzeichen-, marken- oder patentrechtlichem Schutz bzw. sind Warenzeichen oder eingetragene Warenzeichen der jeweiligen Inhaber. Die Wiedergabe von Marken, Produktnamen, Gebrauchsnamen, Handelsnamen, Warenbezeichnungen u.s.w. in diesem Werk berechtigt auch ohne besondere Kennzeichnung nicht zu der Annahme, dass solche Namen im Sinne der Warenzeichen- und Markenschutzgesetzgebung als frei zu betrachten wären und daher von jedermann benutzt werden dürften.

Verlag: Südwestdeutscher Verlag für Hochschulschriften Aktiengesellschaft & Co. KG
Dudweiler Landstr. 99, 66123 Saarbrücken, Deutschland
Telefon +49 681 37 20 271-1, Telefax +49 681 37 20 271-0, Email: info@svh-verlag.de
Zugl.: Darmstadt, TU, Diss.,2009

Herstellung in Deutschland:
Schaltungsdienst Lange o.H.G., Berlin
Books on Demand GmbH, Norderstedt
Reha GmbH, Saarbrücken
Amazon Distribution GmbH, Leipzig
ISBN: 978-3-8381-0787-5

Imprint (only for USA, GB)
Bibliographic information published by the Deutsche Nationalbibliothek: The Deutsche Nationalbibliothek lists this publication in the Deutsche Nationalbibliografie; detailed bibliographic data are available in the Internet at http://dnb.d-nb.de.
Any brand names and product names mentioned in this book are subject to trademark, brand or patent protection and are trademarks or registered trademarks of their respective holders. The use of brand names, product names, common names, trade names, product descriptions etc. even without a particular marking in this works is in no way to be construed to mean that such names may be regarded as unrestricted in respect of trademark and brand protection legislation and could thus be used by anyone.

Publisher:
Südwestdeutscher Verlag für Hochschulschriften Aktiengesellschaft & Co. KG
Dudweiler Landstr. 99, 66123 Saarbrücken, Germany
Phone +49 681 37 20 271-1, Fax +49 681 37 20 271-0, Email: info@svh-verlag.de

Copyright © 2009 by the author and Südwestdeutscher Verlag für Hochschulschriften Aktiengesellschaft & Co. KG and licensors
All rights reserved. Saarbrücken 2009

Printed in the U.S.A.
Printed in the U.K. by (see last page)
ISBN: 978-3-8381-0787-5

ii

Contents

1 Introduction — 1
  1.1 Outline of this Thesis — 2

2 Noise, Variability, and Time-Delayed Feedback — 3
  2.1 Noise and Variability — 4
  2.2 Time-Delayed Feedback — 6
  2.3 Numerical Integration of Stochastic Differential Equations — 7

3 The Model Systems — 9
  3.1 The FitzHugh-Nagumo Model — 10
    3.1.1 Temporal Dynamics of the FitzHugh-Nagumo Model — 10
  3.2 The Hodgkin-Huxley Model — 15
    3.2.1 Temporal Dynamics of the Hodgkin-Huxley Model — 17
  3.3 Net Dynamics — 19
  3.4 Noise and Variability in Nets of FitzHugh-Nagumo Elements — 21

4 Theoretical Tools — 23
  4.1 The Small-Noise Expansion — 23
  4.2 The Effective Parameter c_{eff} — 24
  4.3 Data Analysis — 25

5 Time-Delayed Feedback Control of Oscillatory Neuronal Dynamics — 29
  5.1 Net of FitzHugh-Nagumo Elements with Time-Delayed Feedback — 29
    5.1.1 Influence of Time-Delayed Feedback on a Single Element — 30
    5.1.2 Suppression of Global Oscillation in a Net — 34
  5.2 Oscillatory Hodgkin-Huxley Elements — 42
    5.2.1 Influence of Time-Delayed Feedback on a Single Element — 42
    5.2.2 Suppression of Global Oscillation in a Net — 44

6 Delay-Sustained Pattern Formation in Subexcitable Media — 47
  6.1 Subexcitable Net of FitzHugh-Nagumo Elements — 48
    6.1.1 Time-Delayed Feedback Control of Wave Fronts Induced by Special Initial Conditions — 49
    6.1.2 Time-Delayed Feedback Control of Noise-Induced Pattern Formation — 53
    6.1.3 Time-Delayed Feedback Control of Variability-Induced Pattern Formation — 58

6.2 Subexcitable Net of Hodgkin-Huxley Elements 61

7 Influence of Variability and Noise on the Net Dynamics of Bistable FitzHugh-Nagumo Elements 67
 7.1 Dynamics of a Single Element 68
 7.2 Noise- and Variability-Induced Symmetry 70
 7.3 Variability-Induced Resonance 75
 7.4 Doubly Variability-Induced Resonance 77
 7.5 Influence of Time-Delayed Feedback on Bistable FitzHugh-Nagumo Elements 81

8 Summary and Outlook 87

Zusammenfassung 91

Bibliography 93

Danksagung 101

Chapter 1

Introduction

Many spatially extended, nonlinear systems show complex dynamics in time and space. There are a number of examples for pattern formation in physics, chemistry and biology [1, 2, 3, 4]. Since A. M. Turing in 1952 [5], pattern forming processes are studied intensely. The richness of patterns in nature is due to the nonlinear interaction of the components of the systems. Modeling biological systems, besides the nonlinearities one often has to deal with stochastic influences. Because of the scale (molecular size) of many biological processes, noise can not be neglected. But noise does not always disturb the dynamics of a system, on the contrary, there are several examples where noise has a constructive influence on a system and enhances its functionality [6, 7, 8]. Noise can cause phase transitions [9, 10], favor signal transmission [11, 12], or induce patterns [13]. One of the most impressive and well-studied phenomena of the constructive influence of noise is the stochastic resonance effect [14, 15]. For instance, the paddle fish takes the advantage of stochastic resonance to detect its prey [7]. Noise has also a great impact on the human nervous system [8, 16]. It is shown that the walking pattern of Parkinson patients is significantly improved using stochastic impulses to exercise the coordination [16]. Generally, a good overview on the influence of noise on spatially extended systems is given by J. García-Ojalvo et al. [10] and F. Sagues et al. [13].

Besides noise, variability is omnipresent in nature. Variability (diversity, heterogeneity) denotes time-independent stochastic differences between otherwise equal elements of a system. In the human nervous system for example, each neuron has a slightly different resting potential and/or excitation threshold, which might have a deep impact on the functionality of neural tissues. It is shown that variability crucially influences pattern forming processes [17, 18, 19], synchronization processes [20], or stochastic resonance effects [21, 22, 23].

Nonlinear systems subjected to noise and variability can show a very complex behavior. It is often desirable to be able to control the dynamics of such a system. One generic method to control complex dynamical behavior is the time-delayed feedback scheme introduced by Pyragas to stabilize periodic orbits embedded in a chaotic attractor [24]. Recently, based on the idea of Pyragas, time-delayed feedback was used to suppress the pulse propagation in a chain of neural elements [25]. A number of investigations deal with the impact of time-delayed feedback on neural model systems, because it is essential to be able to manipulate the dynamics of neurons to abort neural diseases like Parkinson, tremor, and epilepsy [26, 27, 28, 29, 30].

All these phenomena motivate the study of spatially extended systems of neural elements under the influence of noise, variability, and time-delayed feedback. Besides detailed numerical investigations, analytical calculations are done. The control of spatially extended systems via time-delayed feedback is a quite new aspect in physics and might reveal interesting results. Besides the feedback control of deterministic systems, the interplay of feedback and noise in pattern forming processes is addressed in this work.

1.1 Outline of this Thesis

In this thesis, the influence of noise, variability, and time-delayed feedback on spatially extended systems is investigated. First noise and variability are characterized and two types of feedback control are introduced in chapter 2. The difference between additive and multiplicative stochastic terms is explained. The model systems under consideration are spatially extended systems of FitzHugh-Nagumo and Hodgkin-Huxley elements, respectively. The model equations and their dynamics are discussed in detail in chapter 3. Besides the temporal dynamics of a single element, the spatiotemporal dynamics of nets is displayed and the noise and variability terms are included in the model equations. In chapter 4, theoretical approaches to estimate the influence of multiplicative stochastic terms are presented. Besides that, a couple of quantities, which serve as order parameters to discern the different dynamical features, are introduced. In the next three chapters (chapters 5- 7), the results are displayed.

In chapter 5, the influence of time-delayed feedback on oscillatory systems is investigated. The influence on a single FitzHugh-Nagumo element is studied first, then nets of FitzHugh-Nagumo elements are considered. In the next section, the results obtained for Hodgkin-Huxley elements are presented. Throughout chapter 6, subexcitable nets are considered. First, the influence of time-delayed feedback on the propagation of wave fronts and pattern formation is examined for the FitzHugh-Nagumo model. In consecutive subsections, the interplay of time-delayed feedback and additive noise, and of time-delayed feedback and additive variability are investigated. Then, the influence of time-delayed feedback on the propagation of wave fronts in subexcitable nets of Hodgkin-Huxley elements is studied. Chapter 7 deals with nets of bistable FitzHugh-Nagumo elements. After an introduction to bistable net dynamics, the influence of multiplicative noise and multiplicative variability on the net dynamics is discussed in section 7.2. In the next two sections, additionally a weak external signal is considered and the influence of additive noise, additive variability, and multiplicative variability on the response of the net to the signal (stochastic resonance effect) is investigated. At the end of chapter 7, the influence of time-delayed feedback on stochastic resonance is studied. Finally in chapter 8, a brief summery and an outlook regarding further research are given.

Chapter 2

Noise, Variability, and Time-Delayed Feedback

The influence of noise and variability, which are omnipresent in nature, on nonlinear spatially extended systems has been a topic of great interest during the last decades. It is well-known that noise, which is a fast stochastic process, does not always increase disorder. On the contrary, it can play a constructive role in many nonlinear systems. Examples are: *Noise-induced phase transitions*, where the transition is observed at a certain noise strength [9, 10]; *stochastic resonance*, where the response of a nonlinear system to an external signal shows a resonance-like dependency on the noise strength [14]; *coherence resonance* (or *stochastic coherence*), where the output of a nonlinear system is most coherent at a certain noise strength [31]; *spatiotemporal stochastic resonance*, where the patterns of spatially extended systems are most coherent or regular at intermediate noise strengths [32, 33]. Furthermore, noise strongly effects the synchronization in excitable and oscillatory systems [20, 34].

In contrast to noise, internal variability denotes time-independent stochastic differences between the otherwise equal elements of a spatially extended system. Similar to noise, variability can play a constructive role. The influence of parameter variability on the synchronization of coupled oscillators is investigated by Winfree [35] and Kuramoto [36]. Variability plays an important role for pattern formation in a net of biochemical oscillators [18]. In some cases, variability acts in a similar manner like noise. For a net of coupled FitzHugh-Nagumo (FHN) [37] elements, it is shown that variability can induce a transition from oscillatory to excitable behavior (*variability-induced transition*) [38, 39]. Variability can also cause resonance-like phenomena, where the response of a net of nonlinear elements to an external signal is maximal at intermediate variability strengths (*diversity-induced resonance*) [21, 22, 23] or where the coherence of variability-induced patterns shows a resonance-like dependency on the variability strength [17]. In other cases, variability and noise can have a completely different impact on pattern formation and synchronization [20].

Besides the influence of stochastic forces, many investigations focus on the control of the dynamics of nonlinear systems. Time-delayed feedback is a widely used method to achieve a qualitative change of the system dynamics. Pyragas introduced a feedback control method to stabilize an unstable orbit of a chaotic attractor to control deterministic chaos [24]. In the field of control engineering, feedback loops are used to build up complex steerings [40]. In laser systems, the mode selection or the band width of the mode can be tuned using the time-delayed feedback of the light field [41, 42, 43]. In other investigations time-delayed feedback is used to control the coherence of noise-induced oscillations [44, 45], the synchronization of two coupled oscillators [34, 46], or generally the stabilization of an unstable focus [47]. In a net of oscillators, it is shown that time-delay feedback can desynchronize the oscillators [27] or that it can efficiently suppress the oscillation (amplitude death) [29, 48].

There are many more examples, where an external feedback is used to manipulate the system dynamics in a desired manner. Furthermore many systems, especially in biology, have intrinsic feedback loops. In gene regulatory networks, for example, feedback loops are crucial for the mechanism of gene expression [49].

In this chapter, the properties of noise and variability are briefly introduced discussing a general stochastic differential equation of first order. The difference between additive and multiplicative stochastic terms is defined. Furthermore, the two different types of the feedback term used in this thesis are introduced.

2.1 Noise and Variability

Any process in nature is subject to internal and external fluctuations (temperature, environmental conditions). So it is important to model noise with the desired properties. The temporal evolution of a process is given by a set of stochastic differential equations of first order. To simplify matters, here only one differential equation is discussed. Let $\eta(t)$ be a noise term acting on the process, its dynamics may be described by

$$\dot{x}(t) = f(x(t)) + g(x(t))\eta(t), \qquad (2.1)$$

where $f(x(t))$ is the deterministic and $g(x(t))\eta(t)$ the stochastic part of the differential equation. If $g(x(t))$ is a constant, the noise term is additive. If $g(x(t))$ depends on the variable $x(t)$, the noise is called multiplicative noise. The noise term $\eta(t)$ is characterized by its probability distribution, its moments and its correlation function. Because of the central limit theorem, the sum of several stochastic influences can be assumed to be Gaussian distributed. A Gaussian distribution $P(\eta, \sigma_n)$ is completely determined by its mean and its variance, where the variance σ_n^2 defines the noise intensity and the standard deviation σ_n the noise strength, respectively. Throughout this thesis, the mean of the noise terms is vanishing. If the time scale of the noise is much smaller than the relevant time scale of the observed process, the noise can be assumed to be white in time. This assumption is not always valid. The temporal correlation of the noise can absolutely affect the dynamics of a process [50, 51], but for the general investigations presented in this thesis any specific correlation of the noise does not play a crucial role. Regarding a spatially extended system (two dimensional net), consisting of $N \times N$ coupled elements, the stochastic differential equation is given by

$$\dot{x}_{ij}(t) = f(x_{ij}(t)) + g(x_{ij}(t))\eta_{ij}(t) + J_{ij}, \qquad (2.2)$$

where the indices $1 \leq i, j \leq N$ enumerate the elements and J_{ij} denotes a coupling function. The noise term $\eta_{ij}(t)$ is assumed to be uncorrelated in space and time. Hence the

2.1. NOISE AND VARIABILITY

correlation function reads

$$\langle \eta_{ij}(t)\eta_{kl}(t') \rangle = \sigma_n^2 \delta_{ij,kl} \delta(t-t') \,. \tag{2.3}$$

This approximation, which denotes that both the spatial length scales and the time scale of the noise term are much smaller than the relevant scales of the system, is again a practical assumption regarding the subject matter of this thesis. Hence, all simulations are performed using spatially uncorrelated Gaussian white noise.

In contrast to noise, variability denotes time-independent stochastic differences between the otherwise equal elements of a net. For a net without noise, the differential equation with variability reads

$$\dot{x}_{ij}(t) = f(x_{ij}(t)) + \mu_{ij} g(x_{ij}(t)) + J_{ij} \,. \tag{2.4}$$

The parameter values μ_{ij} differ from element to element following an arbitrary statistical distribution, but they are constant in time. In contrast to noise, a dynamic property of a system, variability denotes a static property. Again the variability is called additive, if the function $g(x_{ij}(t))$ is a constant, and multiplicative, if $g(x_{ij}(t))$ depends on $x_{ij}(t)$. The variability in parameter μ is characterized by its probability distribution and its spatial correlation. Without loss of generality, throughout this thesis the probability distribution $P(\mu, \sigma_v)$ is chosen to be Gaussian, where the variance σ_v^2 defines the variability intensity and the standard deviation σ_v the variability strength, respectively. Taking uniformly distributed parameter values, one qualitatively yields the same results. The correlation

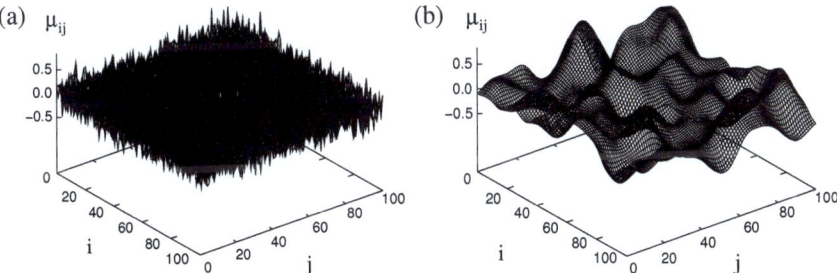

Figure 2.1: *Random distribution (variability) of parameter μ_{ij} of a spatially extended system of 100×100 elements with $\bar{\mu} = \langle \mu_{ij} \rangle_{ij} = 0$ and $\sigma_v = 0.25$. (a) Spatially uncorrelated ($\lambda_\mu = 0.0$). (b) Spatially exponentially correlated ($\lambda_\mu = 5.0$).*

of the parameter distribution is chosen to be either white or exponentially correlated in space. Hence, the correlation function reads

$$\langle (\mu_{ij} - \bar{\mu})(\mu_{kl} - \bar{\mu}) \rangle = \sigma_v^2 \delta_{ij} \delta_{kl} \,, \tag{2.5}$$

for spatially uncorrelated variability, and

$$\langle (\mu_{ij} - \bar{\mu})(\mu_{kl} - \bar{\mu}) \rangle = \sigma_v^2 \exp\left(-\frac{[(i-k)^2 + (j-l)^2]}{\lambda_\mu^2}\right), \tag{2.6}$$

for spatially exponentially correlated variability, respectively. $\bar{\mu}$ denotes the mean value of μ_{ij} and λ_μ the correlation length. In the limit $\lambda_\mu \to 0$, one obtains again a spatially uncorrelated distribution (white variability). The exponentially correlated variability distribution is generated using the spatial frequency filtering method [10, 50]. In Fig. 2.1, two realizations of the distribution of parameter μ are shown for $\sigma_v = 0.25$ and vanishing mean. A spatially uncorrelated distribution ($\lambda_\mu = 0.0$) is plotted in Fig. 2.1 (a), whereas in Fig. 2.1 (b) a strong spatial correlation ($\lambda_\mu = 5.0$) is clearly visible.

2.2 Time-Delayed Feedback

Time-delayed feedback loops are used in many systems in physics, biology, and technics to control the system dynamics. Whereas inherent feedback loops are determined by the systems itself, there exist many different realizations to model external feedback control schemes. A differential equation for a net of $N \times N$ elements with feedback reads

$$\dot{x}_{ij}(t) = f(x_{ij}(t)) + F_{ij}(K, t, \tau). \tag{2.7}$$

Throughout this thesis, two different types of time-delayed feedback $F_{ij}(K, t, \tau)$, also called feedback signal, based on the Pyragas feedback control scheme [24] are applied. Local feedback, given by

$$F_{ij}(K, t, \tau) = K\left[x_{ij}(t-\tau) - x_{ij}(t)\right] g_{ij}, \tag{2.8}$$

denotes that the elements get their own time series fed back. Global feedback is described by

$$F_{ij}(K, t, \tau) = K\left[\langle x_{ij}(t-\tau)\rangle_{ij} - x_{ij}(t)\right] g_{ij}, \tag{2.9}$$

where the mean field time series is fed back. $\langle x_{ij}(t)\rangle_{ij}$ is the spatial average $\bar{x}$ over all elements [Eq. (3.14)]. K denotes the feedback strength and τ the delay time. The matrix element g_{ij} is either equal to one or equal to zero to select the elements that get the feedback signal. The quota g_f of elements that get the feedback signal is given by

$$g_f = \sum_{i,j=1}^{N} \frac{g_{ij}}{N^2}, \tag{2.10}$$

whose value ranges from zero to one. The parameters K, τ, and g_f are denoted as *feedback parameters* for brevity. The feedback control schemes [Eq. (2.8) and Eq. (2.9)] are non-invasive in that sense that the feedback signal vanishes, if the system remains in a spatially homogeneous temporally constant solution. Because of this non-invasiveness, it is reasonable to use feedback of the Pyragas type to control the dynamics of neural networks, which is the main interest of the present studies. Nevertheless, other feedback control schemes, e.g. nonlinear ones [28], are conceivable and absolutely practicable.

The selection of elements that get the feedback signal is either based on a spatially uncorrelated Gaussian random distribution [Fig. 2.1(a)] or on spatially exponentially correlated Gaussian distributed parameter values μ_{ij} [Fig. 2.1(b)] with the correlation length λ_μ [Eq. (2.6)]. For a given realization of μ_{ij} and a fixed value of g_f, the ij-element gets the feedback signal, if $\mu_{ij} < \alpha$ with $H(\mu_{ij} < \alpha) = g_f$, where H denotes the

2.3 NUMERICAL INTEGRATION

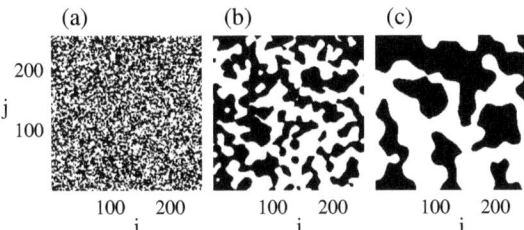

Figure 2.2: *The matrix elements g_{ij} of a spatially extended system of 256×256 elements for $g_f = 0.5$ and three different values of the correlation length λ_μ. Black denotes $g_{ij} = 1.0$ and white $g_{ij} = 0.0$. (a) $\lambda_\mu = 1.0$, (b) $\lambda_\mu = 5.0$, (c) $\lambda_\mu = 10.0$.*

distribution function of μ_{ij}. For large nets, the threshold value α is determined by $H(\mu_{ij} < \alpha) = \int_{-\infty}^{\alpha} P(\mu, \sigma_v) d\mu = g_f$, the distribution function of the probability distribution $P(\mu, \sigma_v)$. In Fig. 2.2, the matrix elements g_{ij} are plotted for $g_f = 0.5$ and three different values of the correlation length λ_μ. Black denotes $g_{ij} = 1.0$, these elements get the feedback signal, and white denotes $g_{ij} = 0.0$. For larger values of λ_μ, larger clusters of elements get the feedback signal, whereas the total number of elements that get the feedback signal is unchanged ($g_f = 0.5$).

2.3 Numerical Integration of Stochastic Differential Equations

In general, nonlinear differential equations can not be solved analytically. The model equations, which are discussed in this thesis, are numerically integrated on a discrete spatiotemporal grid using the Heun method and the Forward Time Centered Space scheme in time and space, respectively [10]. The integration in space is performed using periodic boundary conditions. Without loss of generality, the spatial distance between neighboring elements is set to one. The Heun algorithm, a numerical integration method of second order, is also suitable to integrate stochastic differential equations.

For lucidity, here only the temporal integration, which is not trivial for stochastic differential equations, is described. Let the dynamics be given by the stochastic differential equation Eq. (2.1)
$$\dot{x}(t) = f(x(t)) + g(x(t))\eta(t).$$
The iteration method for the Heun integration, if the noise term is δ-correlated, is given by
$$x(t + \Delta t) = x(t) + \frac{1}{2}[f(x(t)) + f(\tilde{x}(t))]\Delta t + \frac{1}{2}[g(x(t)) + g(\tilde{x}(t))]\eta(t)\sqrt{\Delta t}, \quad (2.11)$$
whereby $\tilde{x}(t)$ is obtained by the explicit Euler step
$$\tilde{x}(t) = x(t) + f(x(t))\Delta t + g(x(t))\eta(t)\sqrt{\Delta t}. \quad (2.12)$$

The temporal increment is chosen to be $\Delta t = 0.001$, for which the integration converges sufficiently fast within a large region of the parameter space.

Chapter 3

The Model Systems

The models under consideration describe essential parts of the dynamics of neurons. A typical feature of neurons is their excitability. Let the neuron be in its rest state (resting potential of the membrane). An external stimulus which exceeds a certain threshold leads to an excitation event (depolarization of the membrane potential). Ion channels open, and the ion currents cause a large amplitude-spike of the membrane potential (action potential). Further ion currents ensure that the membrane potential reaches its rest state again. During this complex exchange of ions, the neuron can not be excited again. The neuron is in its refractory state. After the refractory time, when the starting point is recovered, the neuron can be stimulated again. The two models discussed in this thesis, the FitzHugh-Nagumo (FHN) model [37] and the Hodgkin-Huxley (HH) model [52], show such a threshold behavior and are well-established models for excitability. Regarding a spatially extended system, a typical feature of excitable media is that wave fronts can propagate through the whole system (e.g. the pulse propagation in neural tissues).

Many other systems in physics, chemistry and biology show excitable dynamics. An excitable system needs three basic ingredients: a rest state, an excited state (threshold behavior) and a refractory state. Taking the forest-fire model [53, 54], for example, the single element, a tree, offers the three necessary states. The full-grown tree represents the excitable rest state. A burning tree is the excited state and the period, until a new tree is regrown, is the refractory state. Regarding the whole forest, a fire spreads out in a wavelike manner through the whole system (excitation wave). Other examples, where excitation waves can be found, are the photosensitive Belousov-Zhabotinsky reaction [55] or colonies of Dictyostelium discoideum [4, 56].

Furthermore both the FHN model and the HH model can show limit cycle oscillations. The FHN model can even exhibit bistability. So the discussed models are suitable to study the influence of noise, variability and time-delayed feedback on different fundamental dynamics.

In this chapter the FHN model, a minimal model for neuronal dynamics, and the HH model, the first phenomenological model of neuronal activity derived to fit experimental data, are introduced and their relation is discussed. First the temporal dynamics of the model equations is studied, before the spatiotemporal dynamics of two-dimensional nets is discussed. Furthermore the noise and variability terms are introduced into the model equations.

3.1 The FitzHugh-Nagumo Model

The FitzHugh-Nagumo (FHN) model, a two variable model, which is based on the Van der Pol oscillator, was introduced by Bonhoeffer to describe the propagation of a current pulse along a wire [57]. Later R. FitzHugh and N. Nagumo did fundamental investigations on the dynamics of the model equations [37, 58]. Deriving a physiological state diagram they showed the strong relation to the Hodgkin-Huxley model and established the FHN model as a minimal model for neuronal dynamics. The model system consists of two coupled differential equations, from which the first one is nonlinear:

$$\begin{aligned} \frac{du}{dt} &= \frac{1}{\epsilon}[u(1-u)(u-a) - v + d], \\ \frac{dv}{dt} &= u - cv + e. \end{aligned} \quad (3.1)$$

The variable $u(t)$ represents the membrane potential of a neuron and the variable $v(t)$ is related to the time-dependent conductivity of the potassium channels in the membrane (gating variable) [59]. The dynamics of $u(t)$ is much faster than that of $v(t)$. The separation of the time scales is realized by the small parameter ϵ ($0 < \epsilon \ll 1$). The time is specified in time units ($t.u.$), where one time unit (1000 integration steps) accords approximately with the oscillation period of a single element. The parameters e and c of the second differential equation determine the threshold, at which the potassium channels open, and how fast this happens (cf. the HH model presented in chapter 3.2). Hence, the influence of the parameters e and c on the system dynamics is studied. The parameters of the first differential equation (ϵ, a, d), which also crucially influence the model dynamics, but do not lead to different dynamical behaviors, are fixed throughout each chapter.

3.1.1 Temporal Dynamics of the FitzHugh-Nagumo Model

Due to the nonlinearity, the dynamics of the FHN model is quite complex. One discerns three fundamentally different dynamical behaviors, namely excitable, oscillatory and bistable dynamics. There exists no analytic solution of Eqs. (3.1), but a linear stability analysis provides a good insight into the system dynamics. First one calculates the nullclines

$$0 = u(1-u)(u-a) - v + d \quad \text{and} \quad 0 = u - cv + e, \quad (3.2)$$

which divide the phase space in different areas of $\frac{du}{dt} \gtreqless 0$ and $\frac{dv}{dt} \gtreqless 0$. The intersection points of the nullclines are the fixed points of the system. According to the choice of the parameter values one, two, or three fixed points exist. Depending on the number of fixed points and their stability, one finds different dynamical regimes. Two different sets of the parameters of the first differential equation are discussed in this thesis. To study excitable and oscillatory dynamics, parameter set 1 is used:

$$(\epsilon, a, d) = (0.01, 0.5, 0.1). \quad (3.3)$$

To study bistable dynamics, parameter set 2 is used:

$$(\epsilon, a, d) = (0.01, 0.5, 0.045). \quad (3.4)$$

3.1. THE FITZHUGH-NAGUMO MODEL

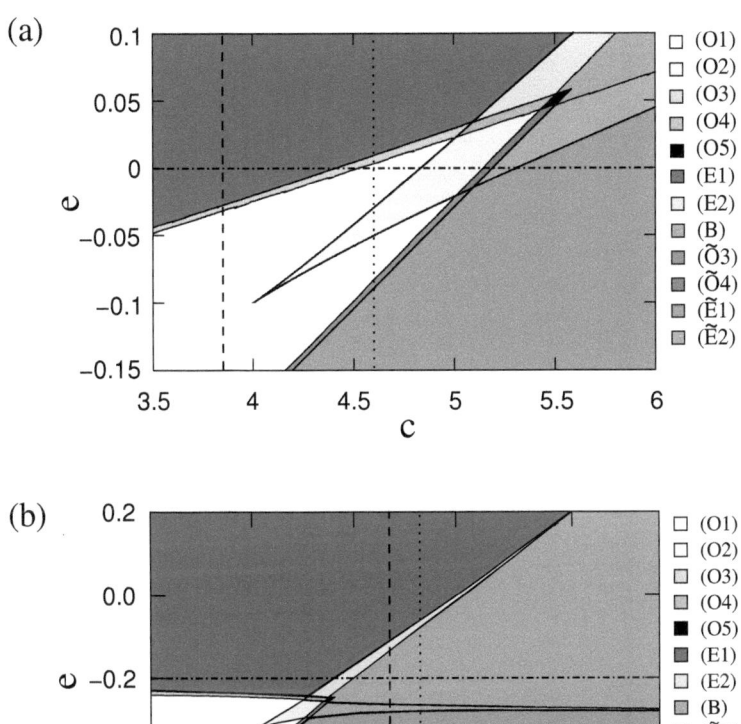

Figure 3.1: *Linear stability analysis of the FHN model [Eqs. (3.1)] dependent on the parameters c and e. (a) For parameter set 1 [Eq. (3.3)], $(- - -)\, c = 3.85$, $(\cdots)\, c = 4.6$, $(-\cdot -)\, e = 0.0$. (b) For parameter set 2 [Eq. (3.4)], $(- - -)\, c = 6.7$, $(\cdots)\, c = 7.3$, $(-\cdot -)\, e = -0.2$. The different dynamical regimes are explained in the text.*

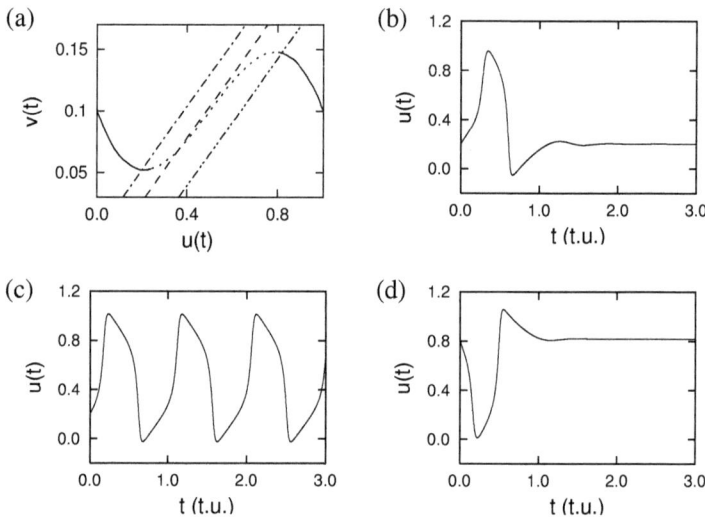

Figure 3.2: (a) Nullclines of the FHN model [Eqs. (3.1)] for parameter set 1, $c = 3.85$, and three different values of e. $(-\cdot-)$ $e = 0.0$, $(---)$ $e = -0.1$, $(-\cdot\cdot-)$ $e = -0.25$. $(—)$ Stable branches of the cubic nullcline, $(\cdots)$ unstable branch of the cubic nullcline. (b), (c), (d) The corresponding time series to the three different parameter values of e. (b) $e = 0.0$, the regime $E1$. (c) $e = -0.1$, the regime $O1$. (d) $e = -0.25$, the regime $\tilde{E}1$.

For both cases a linear stability analysis is performed dependent on the parameters c and e. The results are plotted in Fig. 3.1 (a) for parameter set 1 and in Fig. 3.1 (b) for parameter set 2. The qualitative result of the linear stability analyses is the same for both parameter sets. Changing the parameters a and d only leads to a shift and tilt of the stability diagram, but the same bifurcations and dynamical regimes are found. One can discern three fundamentally different dynamics: Oscillatory dynamics, excitable dynamics and bistable dynamics.

- The regime $O1$: One finds an unstable focus surrounded by a stable limit cycle. After a transient the FHN system performs autonomous limit cycle oscillations, hence this regime is called oscillatory regime. In Fig. 3.2 (c), a time series of the limit cycle motion is shown. The amplitude and the frequency of the oscillation vary only slightly with the parameters c and e.

- The regime $E1$: The only attractor is a stable focus. Without perturbations the trajectory will always run into this fixed point and rest there for all times [Fig. 3.2 (b)]. A perturbation, which drives the system beyond a certain threshold, leads to a large excursion through the phase space (spike in the time series) before the trajectory returns to the fixed point. These spikes correspond to the action potentials of neurons.

3.1. THE FITZHUGH-NAGUMO MODEL

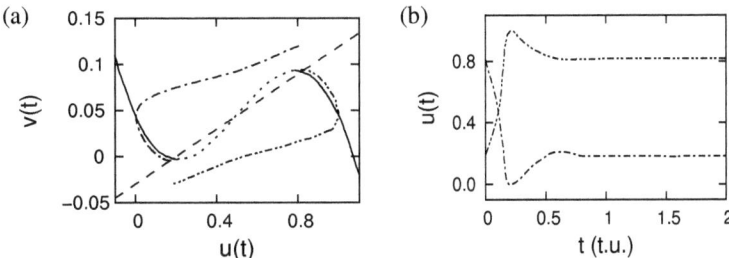

Figure 3.3: *(a) Trajectories in the phase space with nullclines and (b) the corresponding time series for the FHN model [Eqs. (3.1)] for parameter set 2, $c = 6.7$, $e = -0.2$, and two different initial conditions. $(- - -)$ Linear nullcline, $(—)$ stable branches and $(\cdots)$ unstable branch of the cubic nullcline. $(- \cdot -)$ and $(- \cdot \cdot -)$ trajectories and time series, which run into the two different fixed points, respectively.*

Hence, the FHN equations serve as a model for neuronal excitable dynamics. This regime is called excitable regime.

- The regime B: Two stable foci, which are separated by a saddle point, exist. Depending on the initial conditions the trajectory will run into one of the stable foci and rest there for all times [Fig. 3.3]. External perturbations may lead to jumps between the two stable foci (see section 7.1). This regime is called bistable regime.

In between these three main dynamical regimes, small parameter regions exist, where the system shows a more complex behavior. Here the regime $O3$ has to be stressed, because it is important regarding some investigations presented in this thesis. In the regime $O3$, a stable focus and a stable limit cycle coexist. The two attractors are separated by an unstable limit cycle [Figs. 3.4 (a) and 3.4 (b)]. The system can either rest in the stable focus or perform limit cycle oscillations. Hence, the bifurcation from the regime $E1$ to the regime $O1$ is a subcritical Hopf bifurcation. This bifurcation occurs for example by increasing parameter c from 4.3 to 4.6 for parameter set 1 [Eq. (3.3)] and $e = 0.0$ [Fig. 3.1 (a)]. Since the area of attraction of the stable focus in the regime $O3$ is quite small, a perturbation can easily kick the trajectory onto the stable limit cycle. Thus the dynamics of the regime $O3$ is mostly oscillatory in the presence of noise. For the sake of completeness, the other dynamical regimes are briefly described:

- The regime $O2$: This regime shows oscillatory dynamics like $O1$. In difference to the regime $O1$, two unstable foci separated by a saddle point are placed within the stable limit cycle.

- The regime $O4$: Again two attractors, a stable focus and a stable limit cycle, coexist, which are separated by an unstable limit cycle, as for $O3$. But within the stable limit cycle additionally a saddle point and an unstable focus exist.

14 CHAPTER 3. THE MODEL SYSTEMS

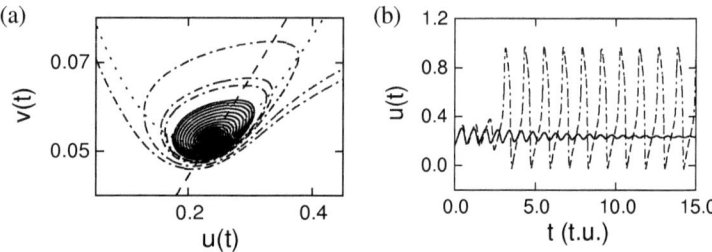

Figure 3.4: (a) Trajectories in the phase space, the vicinity of the stable focus with nullclines, and (b) the corresponding time series for the FHN model [Eq. (3.1)] for parameter set 1, $c = 4.5$, $e = 0.0$, and two different initial conditions. $(- - -)$ Linear nullcline, $(\cdots)$ cubic nullcline. $(- \cdot -)$ Trajectory and time series starting in the area of attraction of the stable limit cycle. $(—)$ Trajectory and time series starting in the area of attraction of the stable focus.

- The regime $O5$: Here two stable foci, where each is surrounded by an unstable limit cycle and which are separated by a saddle point, exist. Additionally, the three fixed points are enclosed by a stable limit cycle. The system performs limit cycle oscillations or remains in one of the stable foci.

- The regime $E2$: As for $E1$, a stable focus is the only attractor. But additionally, a saddle point and an unstable focus exist.

The almost symmetric structure of the stability diagrams [Figs. 3.1 (a) and 3.1 (b)] is based on the symmetry of the cubic nullcline, which can be divided into three branches. Let the linear nullcline be steep enough, so that only one fixed point exists [e.g. for parameter set 1 and $c = 3.85$, Fig. 3.2 (a)]. Varying parameter e, the stability of the fixed point (focus) changes. One finds two branches of the cubic nullcline, where the focus is stable [solid lines in Fig. 3.2 (a)], and in between a branch, where the focus is unstable [dotted line in Fig. 3.2 (a)]. The range of the unstable branch differs only slightly with parameter c. If the stable focus is placed at the left stable branch of the the cubic nullcline, this fixed point is called lower stable fixed point. And the fixed point placed at the right stable branch of the cubic nullcline, is called upper stable fixed point. In all dynamical regimes, which are discussed so far and which have one stable focus, the stable focus is placed at the left stable branch of the the cubic nullcline. The corresponding dynamical regimes, where the stable focus is placed at the right stable branch of the cubic nullcline, are denoted as $\tilde{O}3$, $\tilde{O}4$, $\tilde{E}1$ [Fig. 3.2 (d)], and $\tilde{E}2$, respectively.

The oscillatory state physiologically means that the neuron is permanently spiking. Regarding neuronal diseases, like epilepsy, Parkinson, and tremor, this state depicts the malfunction of a neuron, whereas the excitable state, which allows for information transmission, mimics the healthy neuron. To gain a better understanding of the excitable behavior, a trajectory in the phase space and the corresponding time series of the FHN

3.2. THE HODGKIN-HUXLEY MODEL

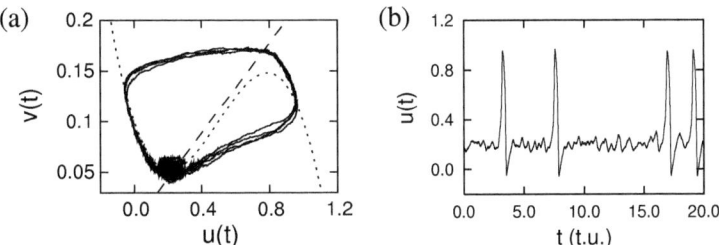

Figure 3.5: *(a) Trajectory in the phase space with nullclines and (b) the corresponding time series for the FHN model [Eq. (3.1)] for parameter set 1, $c = 3.85$, and $e = 0.0$. Weak additive noise ($\sigma_n = 0.01$) is applied to the slow variable $v(t)$. (− − −) Linear nullcline, (· · ·) cubic nullcline. (—) Trajectory and time series, respectively.*

system in the regime $E1$ driven by additive noise are displayed in Figs. 3.5 (a) and 3.5 (b), respectively. Due to the noise, the trajectory fluctuates around the stable focus. If the noise drives the trajectory beyond a certain threshold, the system performs a loop through the phase space before it returns to the vicinity of the stable focus. The noise randomly excites the element (spikes in the time series), whereas the shape and the duration of an excitation spike are hardly affected by the noise.

3.2 The Hodgkin-Huxley Model

The second model discussed in this thesis is the Hodgkin-Huxley (HH) model [52]. Based on measurements of the ion currents through the membrane of squid giant axons, in 1952 A. Hodgkin and A. Huxley derived a phenomenological four variable model to describe excitations in nerve. The current through voltage-gated ion channels in the membrane is mainly composed of a sodium current (index Na) and a potassium current (index K), which are responsible for changing the membrane potential (depolarization). The full HH model consists of one differential equation for the membrane potential $V(t)$ and three differential equations for the gating variables $n(t)$, $m(t)$, and $h(t)$:

$$\begin{aligned}
\frac{dV}{dt} &= [I - g_{Na}m^3h(V - V_{Na}) - g_K n^4(V - V_K) - g_L(V - V_L)]/C\,, \\
\frac{dn}{dt} &= \alpha_n(V)(1 - n) - \beta_n(V)n\,, \\
\frac{dm}{dt} &= \alpha_m(V)(1 - m) - \beta_m(V)m\,, \\
\frac{dh}{dt} &= \alpha_h(V)(1 - h) - \beta_h(V)h\,,
\end{aligned} \quad (3.5)$$

where the functions $\alpha_i(V)$ and $\beta_i(V)$, with $i \in (n, m, h)$, which are fitted to the experimental results, determine the gating characteristics of the ion channels:

$$\begin{aligned}
\alpha_n(V) &= [0.01(V+55)]/\{1-\exp[-(V+55)/10]\}\,,\\
\beta_n(V) &= 0.125\exp[-(V+65)/80]\,,\\
\alpha_m(V) &= [0.1(V+40)]/\{1-\exp[-(V+40)/10]\}\,,\\
\beta_m(V) &= 4\exp[-(V+65)/18]\,,\\
\alpha_h(V) &= 0.07\exp[-(V+65)/20]\,,\\
\beta_h(V) &= 1/\{1+\exp[-(V+35)/10]\}\,.
\end{aligned} \quad (3.6)$$

The membrane potential is measured in mV, the current densities in $\frac{\mu A}{cm^2}$, and the time in ms. Throughout this thesis, it is not crucial to discern between currents and current densities. Thus, the current densities are just denominated as currents or input currents for simplicity. Besides the sodium and potassium currents, a small leakage current (index L) is assumed to account for all other ions (e.g. chloride). g_{Na}, g_K, and g_L denote the maximal conductances of the corresponding ion channels and V_{Na}, V_K, and V_L are the equilibrium potentials. I represents an external current and C is the capacity of the membrane.

Throughout this thesis, the following values of the constants are used:

$$\begin{aligned}
g_{Na} &= 120\frac{mmho}{cm^2}\,,\quad g_K = 36\frac{mmho}{cm^2}\,,\quad g_L = 0.3\frac{mmho}{cm^2}\,,\\
V_{Na} &= 50mV\,,\quad V_K = -77mV\,,\quad V_L = -54.4mV\,,\\
C &= 1\frac{\mu F}{cm^2}\,,
\end{aligned} \quad (3.7)$$

whereas the parameter I is varied. The values of the constants are experimentally found for 6.3°C.

The full Hodgkin-Huxley model can be reduced to a set of two differential equations [59, 60]. The resulting model is called the reduced Hodgkin-Huxley model. Since $m(t)$ evolves much faster than $n(t)$ and $h(t)$, the gating variable $m(t)$ can be eliminated adiabatically. That means that the variable $m(t)$ in the first differential equation is replaced by its stationary solution, i.e. $d_t m(t) = 0$. It reads

$$m_{st}(V) = \frac{\alpha_m(V)}{\alpha_m(V) + \beta_m(V)}\,. \quad (3.8)$$

A second approximation is based on numerical findings. Although there is no mathematical or biological reason, the following assumption holds quite well:

$$n(t) + h(t) \approx 0.8\,. \quad (3.9)$$

Replacing $h(t)$ in the first differential equation, using $h(t) = 0.8 - n(t)$, and with the adiabatic elimination of $m(t)$, one obtains the reduced Hodgkin-Huxley model:

$$\begin{aligned}
\frac{dV}{dt} &= [I - g_{Na}m_{st}^3(0.8-n)(V-V_{Na}) - g_K n^4(V-V_K) - g_L(V-V_L)]/C\,,\\
\frac{dn}{dt} &= \alpha_n(V)(1-n) - \beta_n(V)n\,.
\end{aligned} \quad (3.10)$$

3.2. THE HODGKIN-HUXLEY MODEL

The reduced HH model [Eqs. (3.10)] can be handled much easier analytically and numerically than the full HH model [Eqs. (3.5)]. If statements are addressed to both, the full and the reduced HH model, the plural *HH models* is used. In the next subsection, it is shown that the HH models exhibit excitable and oscillatory dynamics, as the FHN model.

3.2.1 Temporal Dynamics of the Hodgkin-Huxley Model

In dependency on the input current I, a linear stability analysis is performed for both the full and reduced HH model. The results are displayed in Fig. 3.6. One finds the excitable regime $E1$ for small values of I, the oscillatory regime $O1$ for large values of I and in between the coexistence of a stable focus and a stable limit cycle (regime $O3$; see section 3.1.1). Increasing parameter I, both models undergo a subcritical Hopf bifurcation, which is also found for the FHN model [cf. Figs. 3.1 (a) and 3.1 (b)]. Since the reduced

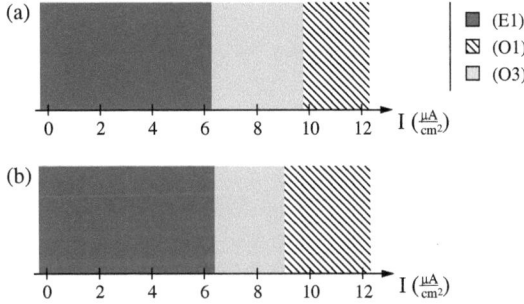

Figure 3.6: *Linear stability analysis of (a) the full Hodgkin-Huxley model [Eqs. (3.5)] and (b) the reduced Hodgkin-Huxley model [Eqs. (3.10)] dependent on the parameter I. (E1) One stable focus, excitable regime. (O1) One unstable focus surrounded by a stable limit cycle, oscillatory regime. (O3) Coexistence of a stable focus and a stable limit cycle.*

HH equations show the same dynamics as the full HH equations, the assumptions used for the reduction of the model equations, are justified at least for the given set of parameters. The parameter region of I, where the two attractors coexist, is only slightly larger for the full HH model than for the reduced HH model. For other parameter values, the full and reduced model can show different bifurcations [19].

In Fig. 3.7, time series of all four variables of the full HH model are composed. For $I = 4.5 \frac{\mu A}{cm^2}$, the only attractor is a stable focus (regime $E1$). Without perturbations, the trajectory runs into this fixed point and rests there for all times [Fig. 3.7 (a)]. A larger input current ($I = 10.0 \frac{\mu A}{cm^2}$) excites the HH system permanently, thus it performs autonomous limit cycle oscillations [regime $O1$, Fig. 3.7 (b)].

The corresponding time series for the reduced HH model look very similar. Since the reduced model contains only two variables, it is easily possible to regard the dynamics in phase space. In Fig. 3.8 (a), a phase space plot with nullclines is shown for $I = 4.5 \frac{\mu A}{cm^2}$. Again the only attractor is a stable focus (regime $E1$). For $I = 10.0 \frac{\mu A}{cm^2}$, the focus is

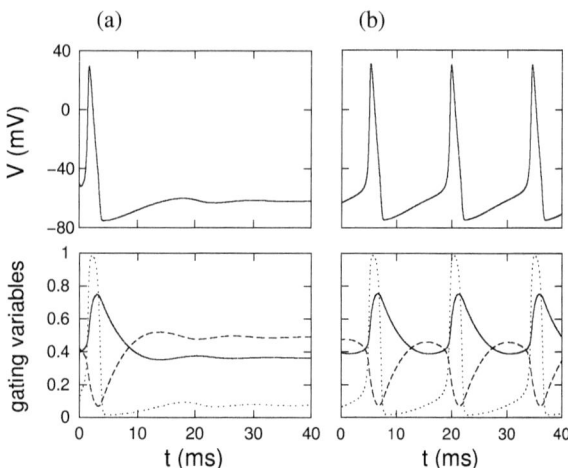

Figure 3.7: *Time series of the membrane potential $V(t)$ (first row) and the gating variables $n(t)$, $m(t)$, and $h(t)$ (second row) for the full HH model [Eq. (3.5)]. (—) $n(t)$, ($\cdots$) $m(t)$, and (– – –) $h(t)$. (a) $I = 4.5 \frac{\mu A}{cm^2}$ [excitable regime (E1)]. (b) $I = 10.0 \frac{\mu A}{cm^2}$ [oscillatory regime (O1)].*

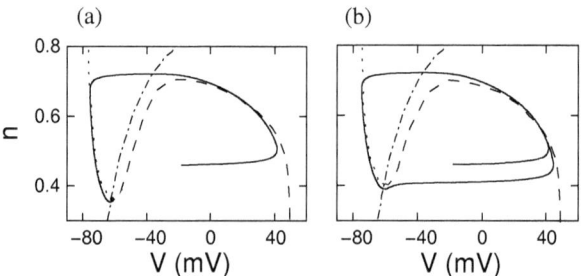

Figure 3.8: *Trajectory in the phase space with nullclines for the reduced HH model [Eq. (3.10)]. (–·–) the n-nullcline ($dn/dt = 0$), ($\cdots$) stable branch and (– – –) unstable branch of the V-nullcline ($dV/dt = 0$). (a) (—) Trajectory for $I = 4.5 \frac{\mu A}{cm^2}$ [excitable regime (E1)]. (b) (—) Trajectory for $I = 10 \frac{\mu A}{cm^2}$ [oscillatory regime (O1)].*

unstable, but a stable limit cycle exists. In Fig. 3.8 (b), the limit cycle trajectory is plotted in phase space (regime $O1$). In both panels the dashed-dotted line marks the n-nullcline, where $dn/dt = 0$ is valid. The V-nullcline ($dV/dt = 0$) is separated into a stable branch (dotted line) and an unstable branch (dashed line). In comparison to the FHN model, one discerns that a linearization of the n-nullcline results in the linear nullcline of the FHN equations [Eqs. 3.1] and that the cubic nullcline of the FHN equations can be seen as an approximation of the V-nullcline. This consideration explains qualitatively the close relation between the dynamics of the HH model and the FHN model.

The main difference between the dynamics of the HH models and the FHN model is that the bistable regime only exists for the FHN model. The cubic nullcline of the FHN equations has two stable branches, which are responsible for the existence of the bistable dynamics. Since the V-nullcline of the HH equations has only one stable branch regarding the given gating variables within a reasonable range of parameter values, the existence of two stable fixed points is impossible.

3.3 Net Dynamics

In this thesis, the focus is on investigations of the dynamics of spatially extended systems. Arranging $N \times N$ coupled elements on a square grid with the side length N, one obtains different regular nets. The dynamics of the single elements is given by the model equations (3.1), (3.5), or (3.10), respectively. The elements are labeled by the indices i and j, which run from one to N. The model equations for the two dimensional nets read:

- for a net of FHN elements:

$$\begin{aligned}
\frac{du_{ij}}{dt} &= \frac{1}{\epsilon}[u_{ij}(1-u_{ij})(u_{ij}-a) - v_{ij} + d] + D_u J_{ij}, \\
\frac{dv_{ij}}{dt} &= u_{ij} - cv_{ij} + e,
\end{aligned} \qquad (3.11)$$

- for a net of HH elements (full model):

$$\begin{aligned}
\frac{dV_{ij}}{dt} &= [I - g_{Na}m_{ij}^3 h_{ij}(V_{ij} - V_{Na}) \\
&\quad - g_K n_{ij}^4 (V_{ij} - V_K) - g_L(V_{ij} - V_L)]/C + D_V J_{ij}, \\
\frac{dn_{ij}}{dt} &= \alpha_n(V_{ij})(1-n_{ij}) - \beta_n(V_{ij})n_{ij}, \\
\frac{dm_{ij}}{dt} &= \alpha_m(V_{ij})(1-m_{ij}) - \beta_m(V_{ij})m_{ij}, \\
\frac{dh_{ij}}{dt} &= \alpha_h(V_{ij})(1-h_{ij}) - \beta_h(V_{ij})h_{ij},
\end{aligned} \qquad (3.12)$$

- for a net of reduced HH elements:

$$\begin{aligned}
\frac{dV_{ij}}{dt} &= [I - g_{Na}m_{ij,st}^3(0.8 - n_{ij})(V_{ij} - V_{Na}) \\
&\quad - g_K n_{ij}^4(V_{ij} - V_K) \quad g_L(V_{ij} - V_L)]/C + D_V J_{ij}, \\
\frac{dn_{ij}}{dt} &= \alpha_n(V_{ij})(1-n_{ij}) - \beta_n(V_{ij})n_{ij}.
\end{aligned} \qquad (3.13)$$

The function J_{ij} denotes the coupling function and the constant D_x denotes the coupling strength, which is considered to be spatially independent throughout this thesis. The index x represents the variables u or V, respectively. Nets with two different types of coupling are investigated. One type is the mean field coupling (global coupling), where each element is coupled to the spatial mean of all elements. Thus the coupling function reads:

$$J_{ij} = \bar{x} - x_{ij}, \qquad \bar{x} = \frac{1}{N^2} \sum_{i,j=1}^{N} x_{ij}. \qquad (3.14)$$

The other type is diffusive, nearest-neighbor coupling (local coupling), where each element is connected with its eight nearest neighbors. The coupling function results from the discretization of the Laplacian operator (nine-point discretization):

$$\begin{aligned} J_{ij} &= \nabla^2 x_{ij}, \\ \nabla^2 x_{ij} &= \frac{1}{6}[x_{i+1,j+1} + x_{i+1,j-1} + x_{i-1,j+1} + x_{i-1,j-1} \\ &\quad + 4(x_{i+1,j} + x_{i-1,j} + x_{i,j+1} + x_{i,j-1}) - 20 x_{ij}]. \end{aligned} \qquad (3.15)$$

Whereas the global coupling enforces spatially homogeneous net dynamics, the diffusive coupling allows to study pattern formation, traveling waves and signal transmission through the net. Throughout this thesis, the net size N is always sufficiently large so that the spatial structures emerge independently of the specific size of the net. In this section, also the coupling strength, which generally has a crucial influence on the spatiotemporal dynamics, is sufficiently large to ensure coherent pattern formation.

In Fig. 3.9, snapshots of the variable $u_{ij}(t)$ of a net of FHN elements are composed for different consecutive times t to show the temporal evolution of the most important dynamical regimes of a deterministic, diffusively coupled net. The variable $u_{ij}(t)$ is encoded in gray scales, where white denotes the minimal amplitude ($u_{ij}(t) \leq -0.2$) and black the maximal amplitude ($u_{ij}(t) \geq 1.2$). In between the gray scale is linearly interpolated. The simulations are done for parameter set 1. Other parameters are $e = 0.0$, $N = 256$, and $D_u = 50$. Different values of parameter c, and different initial conditions are chosen.

For $c = 4.6$, the single elements are oscillating (regime $O1$). Starting with random initial conditions, after a transient all elements oscillate synchronously [global oscillation, Fig. 3.9 (a)]. Due to the strong coupling, initial phase differences between the single elements vanish quickly. Besides the global oscillation of the net, stable traveling wave solutions are possible. But they have a very small area of attraction compared with the global oscillation. Thus starting with random initial conditions, one will almost always end up with globally synchronized oscillations.

For $c = 4.2$, the single elements are excitable (regime $E1$). In Fig. 3.9 (b), a time series of snapshots of $u_{ij}(t)$ is shown starting with random initial conditions. The trajectory of each element runs into the stable focus and rests there for all times. The spatially homogeneous temporally constant solution is stable. Applying special initial conditions, wave fronts can be induced. In Fig. 3.9 (c), the evolution of a spiral wave, which is another stable solution of excitable net dynamics ($c = 4.2$), is shown. The typical feature of an excitable medium is that excitation waves can propagate through the whole medium. For $c = 3.85$, the single elements are excitable as well (regime $E1$), but the excitation wave

2.3 NOISE AND VARIABILITY IN NETS OF FHN ELEMENTS

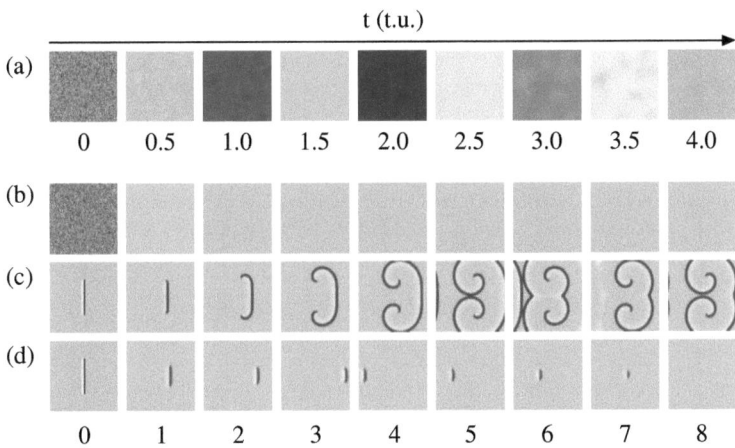

Figure 3.9: *Snapshots of the variable $u_{ij}(t)$ of a net of FHN elements [Eqs. (3.11)] for different consecutive times t. $u_{ij}(t)$ is encoded in gray scales: White denotes $u_{ij}(t) \leq -0.2$, black $u_{ij}(t) \geq 1.2$, with linear interpolation. (a) Random initial conditions, $c = 4.6$: Global oscillation. (b) Random initial conditions, $c = 4.2$: Excitable regime, all elements rest in the stable focus. (c) Special initial conditions, $c = 4.2$: Excitable regime, spiral wave. (d) Special initial conditions, $c = 3.85$: Subexcitable regime, the excitation wave dies out. Further parameters: Parameter set 1, $e = 0.0$, $N = 256$ and $D_u = 50$.*

dies out [Fig. 3.9 (d)]. If all excitation waves die out, the net is called subexcitable. The spatially homogeneous, temporally constant solution is the only stable solution of the net. The propagation of wave fronts is not sustained.

For a net of HH elements [Eqs. (3.12) and Eqs. (3.13)], the same dynamical regimes are found. The net can show global oscillations, excitable and subexcitable behavior as described above for nets of FHN elements. For a net of bistable FHN elements, the dynamics is discussed in detail in chapter 7.

3.4 Noise and Variability in Nets of FitzHugh-Nagumo Elements

In this thesis, the influence of noise and variability on the dynamics of nets of FHN elements plays a central role. The stochastic terms are included in the slow variable [variable $v(t)$ of (Eqs. 3.11)]. With additive noise and variability, and multiplicative noise and variability, the model equations read:

$$\begin{aligned}\frac{du_{ij}}{dt} &= \frac{1}{\epsilon}[u_{ij}(1-u_{ij})(u_{ij}-a)-v_{ij}+d]+D_u J_{ij}\,,\\ \frac{dv_{ij}}{dt} &= u_{ij}-c_{ij}(1+\eta_{ij})v_{ij}+e_{ij}+\xi_{ij}\,.\end{aligned} \quad (3.16)$$

Throughout this thesis, the noise terms are chosen to be Gaussian white noise in time and space with vanishing mean. Hence, the additive noise term $\xi_{ij}(t)$ and the multiplicative noise term $\eta_{ij}(t)$ are characterized by

$$\langle\xi_{ij}(t)\rangle = 0\,,\quad \langle\xi_{ij}(t)\xi_{kl}(t')\rangle = \sigma_{n,e}^2 \delta_{ij,kl}\delta(t-t')\,, \quad (3.17)$$
$$\langle\eta_{ij}(t)\rangle = 0\,,\quad \langle\eta_{ij}(t)\eta_{kl}(t')\rangle = \sigma_{n,c}^2 \delta_{ij,kl}\delta(t-t')\,, \quad (3.18)$$

where $\sigma_{n,e}$ denotes the additive noise strength and $\sigma_{n,c}$ the multiplicative noise strength, respectively.

The variability in the parameters e and c is assumed to be spatially uncorrelated. The additive variability term e_{ij} and the multiplicative variability term c_{ij} are characterized by

$$\langle e_{ij}\rangle = E\,,\quad \langle(e_{ij}-E)(e_{kl}-E)\rangle = \sigma_{v,e}^2 \delta_{ij,kl}\,, \quad (3.19)$$
$$\langle c_{ij}\rangle = C\,,\quad \langle(c_{ij}-C)(c_{kl}-C)\rangle = \sigma_{v,c}^2 \delta_{ij,kl}\,, \quad (3.20)$$

where $\sigma_{v,e}$ denotes the additive variability strength and $\sigma_{v,c}$ the multiplicative variability strength, respectively.

As explained in section 3.2, the slow variable $v(t)$ mimics the gating properties of the potassium ion channels. The parameters e and c determine the position and the slope of the linear nullcline, respectively. Hence the additive stochastic terms mean that the value of the membrane potential, at which the ion channels open, varies. Analogous the multiplicative stochastic terms causes differences for the velocity, with which the ion channels open. The noise terms account for temporal fluctuations in the gating properties, whereas the variability terms represent the time-independent differences from element to element in the gating properties.

In contrast to the additive stochastic terms, the multiplicative stochastic terms have a systematic influence on the dynamics of the observed system. A theoretical approach to describe this systematic influence is introduced in the next chapter.

Chapter 4

Theoretical Tools

For the deterministic model equations a linear stability analysis provides a good method to analyse the dynamics of a system. However, in this thesis the FHN model is extended by stochastic terms [Eqs. (3.16)], which are difficult to handle with analytical methods. In this chapter, theoretical approaches are introduced, resulting in deterministic approximations of the stochastic differential equations. These approximated equations again allow a linear stability analysis. Further a couple of data analysis tools to quantify the net dynamics are introduced.

4.1 The Small-Noise Expansion

The small-noise expansion (SNE) is an approved method to estimate the influence of multiplicative noise [10, 61, 62]. Considering the typical stochastic differential equation [Eq. (2.1)], the influence of the multiplicative noise term is based on the fact that the temporal mean $\langle g(x(t))\eta(t)\rangle$ does not vanish, in contrast to additive noise terms. The first order of the SNE reads

$$\dot{x}(t) = f(x(t)) + \langle g(x(t))\eta(t)\rangle, \tag{4.1}$$

which is a pure deterministic equation. Stochastic terms only appear in higher-order terms of this expansion. As the denomination "small-noise expansion" reveals, this approximation is only valid, if the noise strength is small enough. However, for which range of noise strengths this method works, has to be estimated by numerical calculations.

For the special case of Gaussian white noise, the temporal mean $\langle g(x(t))\eta(t)\rangle$ can be calculated explicitly using Novikov's theorem [63] with the Stratonovich interpretation [64]. One obtains

$$\langle g(x(t))\eta(t)\rangle = \frac{1}{2}\sigma_n^2 g(x(t))\frac{dg(x(t))}{dx}. \tag{4.2}$$

Applying this result to the second equation of Eqs. (3.16), where no variability is considered ($\sigma_{v,e} = 0$, $\sigma_{v,c} = 0$), one yields a deterministic approximation of this equation, which reads

$$\frac{dv_{ij}}{dt} = u_{ij} - c(1 - \frac{1}{2}\sigma_{n,c}^2 c)v_{ij} + e. \tag{4.3}$$

Introducing a new bifurcation parameter

$$c_{SNE}(\sigma_{n,c}) = c(1 - \frac{1}{2}\sigma_{n,c}^2 c), \qquad (4.4)$$

one discerns that an increasing noise strength leads to a smaller value of c_{SNE}. Comparing the effective parameter c_{SNE} with the result of the linear stability analysis (Fig. 3.1), one can predict the influence of multiplicative noise on the dynamics of a net. This influence is called *systematic influence* of the multiplicative noise term throughout this thesis.

4.2 The Effective Parameter c_{eff}

Regarding a net of FHN elements with variability in parameter c, the net contains elements of different dynamical regimes. The dynamics of the ij-element is thereby determined by the slope of the linear nullcline $m_{ij} = 1/c_{ij}$ or by the gradient angle of the linear nullcline $\alpha_{ij} = \arctan(1/c_{ij})$, respectively. Analog to the SNE, where a temporal average of the noise term is used to approximate the model equation, now in the case of variability, a spatial average leads to a simplified equation. The mean gradient angle of the linear nullclines of all elements of the net is a macroscopic net parameter that explains the global dynamics of large nets with sufficiently strong coupling [17, 23, 38]. The mean gradient angle is given by

$$\langle \alpha \rangle = \langle \alpha_{ij} \rangle_{ij} = \frac{1}{N^2} \sum_{i,j=1}^{N} \left(\arctan \left(\frac{1}{c_{ij}} \right) \right). \qquad (4.5)$$

For large nets, it can be calculated approximately as

$$\langle \alpha(\sigma_{v,c}) \rangle \approx \int_{-\infty}^{\infty} \arctan\left(\frac{1}{c}\right) P(c, \sigma_{v,c}) dc, \qquad (4.6)$$

where $P(c, \sigma_{v,c})$ denotes the Gaussian probability distribution of parameter c with variance $\sigma_{v,c}^2$. Finally, introducing the effective parameter c_{eff}

$$c_{eff}(\sigma_{v,c}) = \frac{1}{\tan \langle \alpha \rangle}, \qquad (4.7)$$

one ends up with the following set of differential equations

$$\begin{aligned} \frac{du_{ij}}{dt} &= \frac{1}{\epsilon}[u_{ij}(1-u_{ij})(u_{ij}-a) - v_{ij} + d] + D_u J_{ij}, \\ \frac{dv_{ij}}{dt} &= u_{ij} - c_{eff} v_{ij} + e. \end{aligned} \qquad (4.8)$$

Again, comparing the effective parameter c_{eff} with the result of the linear stability analysis (Fig. 3.1), one can predict the influence of multiplicative variability on the net dynamics. This influence is called *systematic influence* of the multiplicative variability term throughout this thesis.

Another method to simplify spatially extended models with multiplicative variability is a mean field approach, where for each system variable a mean variable and a shape parameter are introduced to describe the net dynamics [65, 66].

4.3 Data Analysis

In this section, several measures are introduced, which are used in this thesis to quantify the net dynamics. To proof transitions between different dynamical regimes, the relative rest time and the time-averaged mean-field are reasonable measures. To study pattern formation and signal transmission through the net, the spatial cross correlation and the mutual information, which account for the coherence of the patterns, are used. The linear response is used to quantify the response of the observed system to an external signal. Calculating these measures, a transient of $5\,t.u.$ (regarding the FHN model) or $40\,ms$ (regarding the HH models) is excluded. Furthermore, characteristic measures for an excitation spike and for an excitation wave are defined.

Relative Rest Time

The relative rest time is a measure for the excitability of a system. Regarding the phase space, the observed systems are excitable, if they are in the vicinity of their stable focus (cf. chapter 3). The relative rest time T_r is defined as the time t_r, in which the system rests in the vicinity of the stable focus, normalized by a fixed integration time T:

$$T_r = \frac{t_r}{T}. \tag{4.9}$$

Throughout this thesis the relative rest time is only used for the HH models. For the reduced HH model [Eqs.(3.10)], the following choice of the borders of the vicinity of the focus are used to calculate the relative rest time:

$$V(t) < V_{th} = -55.0\,mV\,,\ n(t) < n_{th} = 0.42\,. \tag{4.10}$$

Within a certain range, the specific choice of the borders V_{th} and n_{th} of the vicinity of the focus has no crucial influence on the result of the relative rest time. For a HH element, obeying the full model equations [Eqs.(3.5)], one obtains reasonable results for the relative rest time demanding the following terms:

$$\begin{aligned}V(t) < V_{th} = -55.0\,mV\,,\ n(t) < n_{th} = 0.42\,,\\ m(t) < m_{th} = 0.09\,,\ h(t) > h_{th} = 0.40\,.\end{aligned} \tag{4.11}$$

Regarding a net, the relative rest time averaged over all elements provides a good measure to determine the excitability of a net.

If all elements rest in their stable focus and no excitations occur, the relative rest time takes its maximum value of 1. If elements get excited, performing loops through the phase space, the relative rest time decreases. In the case of global oscillation, the relative rest time takes its minimum value.

Mean Field

Especially for nets of FHN elements, the time-averaged mean field M provides a good measure to discern different dynamical regimes. Throughout this thesis, the time-averaged mean field of the variable $u_{ij}(t)$ is used:

$$M = \langle u_{ij}(t) \rangle_{ij,T}. \tag{4.12}$$

If all elements rest in the same fixed point, the time-averaged mean field takes the value of the fixed point [$M \approx 0.2$ (lower stable fixed point) or $M \approx 0.8$ (upper stable fixed point)]. In the case of pattern formation or global oscillation, it takes a value in between ($0.35 < M < 0.65$). Regarding a single FHN element, Eq. (4.12) is reduced to the time average $M = \langle u(t) \rangle_T$ of the variable $u(t)$.

For the HH models, the averaged value of $V(t)$ over one oscillation is close to the value of the fixed point. Thus the measure M is not suitable for the HH models.

Spatial Cross Correlation

To quantify the influence of noise, variability, and time-delayed feedback on pattern formation, the spatial cross correlation S is used [33, 67]. Since in this thesis pattern formation is only studied using the FHN model, the measure S is directly introduced for the slow variable $v(t)$ of Eqs. (3.11). The spatial cross correlation is defined as the space and time averaged nearest-neighbor amplitude-distance of all elements [spatial autocovariance $C_a(t)$] normalized by the total spatial amplitude variance $V_a(t)$. The spatial autocovariance of the nearest-neighbors is given by

$$C_a(t) = \frac{1}{N^2} \sum_{ij} \frac{1}{L} \sum_{kl} (v_{ij} - \bar{v})(v_{kl} - \bar{v}), \qquad (4.13)$$

with the indices k and l summing up all $L = 4$ elements of a von Neumann neighborhood at each lattice site. The total spatial amplitude variance is defined as

$$V_a(t) = \frac{1}{N^2} \sum_{ij} (v_{ij} - \bar{v})^2, \quad \bar{v} = \sum_{i,j=1}^{N} v_{ij}. \qquad (4.14)$$

The spatial cross correlation is given by

$$S = \left\langle \frac{C_a(t)}{V_a(t)} \right\rangle_T, \qquad (4.15)$$

where $\langle \ \rangle_T$ stands for averaging over the whole integration time. S is a measure for the relative change of the local order of a spatially extended system. Thus, a larger value of S denotes a greater coherence of the patterns in the net.

Mutual Information

Another measure to quantify the coherence of the net dynamics and the transmitted information through the net is the mutual information I, an information theory-based method [68, 69]. This measure is only used for the FHN model [Eqs. (3.11)]. To calculate the mutual information, the time series of the single FHN elements have to be mapped onto a binary state space, with the states 0 and 1 corresponding to the resting and the excited state, respectively. This mapping is realized using the threshold value $u_{th} = 0.7$. Within a certain range, the specific choice of this threshold value has no influence on the result of the

4.3. DATA ANALYSIS

mutual information. Based on the joint Shannon entropy for several stochastic processes, the mutual information for a net of FHN elements evolving in time can be written as

$$I = \left\langle \frac{1}{L} \sum_{kl} \sum_{q,r \in \{0,1\}} p_{qr}^{ij,kl} \ln\left(\frac{p_{qr}^{ij,kl}}{p_q^{ij} p_r^{kl}}\right) \right\rangle_{ij}, \qquad (4.16)$$

with the indices k and l summing up all $L = 4$ elements of a von Neumann neighborhood at each lattice site. p_q^{ij} is the probability of the ij-element to be in the state $q \in \{0, 1\}$, and $p_{qr}^{ij,kl}$ denotes the joint probability of neighboring elements. The brackets $\langle\ \rangle_{ij}$ stand for averaging over all elements of the net. The mutual information I increases with an increasing interaction between neighboring elements. If one element spikes (signal) and excites a neighboring element (transmission of the signal), these elements strongly interact, which causes a large joint probability, and thus a positive contribution to I. Regarding the whole net, the interaction between the elements provokes the development of wave fronts, which propagate through the net. The value of I increases with the number and the size of the wave fronts. Thus a larger value of I denotes a better signal transmission through the net. The mutual information takes its minimum value zero, if all elements remain in their fixed point (no excitations) or if neighboring elements spike uncorrelated.

Linear Response

To proof the existence of stochastic resonance, the linear response Q provides a suitable measure. Let $x(t)$ be the relevant system variable and $s(t)$ a signal with the fixed frequency ω and amplitude A

$$s(t) = A \cos(\omega t). \qquad (4.17)$$

The linear response Q is the normalized Fourier transformation of $x(t)$ evaluated at the fixed frequency ω. Taking a time series of $x(t)$, Q can be estimated in the following manner [11]:

$$Q = \frac{\omega}{2k\pi A} \left| \int_0^{\frac{2k\pi}{\omega}} 2x(t) e^{(i\omega t)} dt \right|, \qquad (4.18)$$

where k is the number of periods of the signal. Regarding a net, one calculates the linear response of the time series of the mean field $\langle x_{ij}(t) \rangle_{ij}$.

Characteristics of an Excitation Spike

The duration of a whole excitation spike is mainly composed of the duration of the excitation $B(\nu_1, \nu_2)$ and the duration of the refractory period $R(\nu_1, \nu_2)$ [Fig. 4.1 (a)]. For the FHN model, the measure

$$\Delta B = \frac{B(\nu_1, \nu_2)}{B_0} \qquad (4.19)$$

is introduced as the normalized time span of an excitation, for which $u(t) \geq 0.4$ is valid. Analog, the normalized duration of the refractory period ΔR is defined as

$$\Delta R = \frac{R(\nu_1, \nu_2)}{R_0} \quad \text{with} \quad u(t) \leq 0.18. \qquad (4.20)$$

CHAPTER 4. THEORETICAL TOOLS

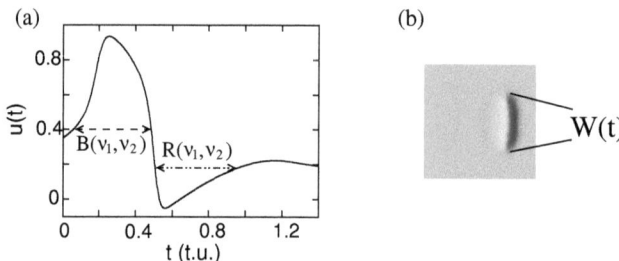

Figure 4.1: (a) Sketch to explain the definition of (− − −) the duration $B(\nu_1, \nu_2)$ of the excitation and (− ·· −) the duration $R(\nu_1, \nu_2)$ of the refractory period of an excitation spike. (b) Sketch to illustrate the definition of the width $W(t)$ of a wave front induced by special initial conditions.

The measures ΔB and ΔR are used in dependency on $(\nu_1, \nu_2) = (c, e)$ or $(\nu_1, \nu_2) = (K, \tau)$. The reference values B_0 and R_0 are taken without feedback for the parameter values $c = 3.85$ and $e = 0.0$, which are chosen for all simulations of subexcitable nets of FHN elements (see chapter 6). For the HH models, only the measure ΔB is used, which is calculated as for the FHN model with the condition $V(t) \geq -30mV$.

Relative Change of the Width of a Wave Front

To determine whether a net shows excitable or subexcitable dynamics, the propagation of a wave front induced by special initial conditions is observed and the relative change of the width of the wave front is used. Therefore, the quotient of the width $W(t_i)$ of the wave front [Fig. 4.1 (b)] at two different times t_i

$$\Delta W = \frac{W(t_2)}{W(t_1)} \quad (4.21)$$

is calculated. For the FHN model, the times t_1 and t_2 are chosen to be $t_1 = 1\,t.u.$ and $t_2 = 4\,t.u.$. For the HH models, $t_1 = 5\,ms$ and $t_2 = 20\,ms$ are used. The time t_1 has to be chosen small enough to ensure that the wave front is not extended over the whole net, but not too close to zero to await the formation of the wave front. The time t_2 is chosen larger than t_1 so that the evolution of the width of the wave front has taken place. $\Delta W > 1$ means that the wave front is growing and the net is excitable, for $\Delta W < 1$ the wave front is shrinking (subexcitable dynamics). This case differentiation is independent of the specific choice of the times t_1 and t_2. However, it is important to mention that the border between subexcitable and excitable net dynamics can not clearly be defined, because the growing or shrinking of a wave front depends also on its initialized shape and thickness. The presented results do not lose their general validity, although the border $\Delta W = 1$ is only exact for the applied initial conditions.

Chapter 5

Time-Delayed Feedback Control of Oscillatory Neuronal Dynamics

Neural systems show a great variety of different dynamics, which can be mostly characterized by an excitable or oscillatory behavior. Synchronized oscillations of an ensemble of neurons is not always desirable, because this regular activity is believed to play a crucial role in the emergence of pathological rhythmic brain activity [26]. Whereas an excitable net allows signal transmission, the propagation of excitation waves through the net (healthy state of a neural tissue), the global oscillation is connected with neuronal malfunction. Rosenblum and Pikovsky [27] showed that the suppression of synchrony in a globally coupled network of oscillators with different frequencies is possible via time-delayed feedback of the mean field. To reach an effective desynchronization of a coupled ensemble of oscillators Popovych et al. [28] suggested to use nonlinear delayed feedback. Other studies focus on the suppression of the global oscillation and the restoration of excitable network dynamics via noise [51, 70] and variability [38, 39] (noise- and variability-induced phase transition).

In this chapter the influence of time-delayed feedback on oscillatory neuronal dynamics is discussed. First, the FHN model is investigated. The dynamics of a single element with time-delayed feedback is studied and the numerical simulations are compared with the result of a linear stability analysis. In a next subsection, the influence of global and local feedback on the dynamics of nets is investigated in detail. Then, the results of the HH models are presented. Throughout this chapter, only diffusively coupled nets [Eq. (3.15)] are considered.

5.1 Net of FitzHugh-Nagumo Elements with Time-Delayed Feedback

The system under consideration is a net of $N \times N$ coupled FHN elements with additive noise extended by a time-delayed feedback loop, which is either introduced in the fast variable $u(t)$

$$\frac{du_{ij}}{dt} = \frac{1}{\epsilon}[u_{ij}(1-u_{ij})(u_{ij}-a) - v_{ij} + d] + F_{ij}(K,t,\tau) + D_u\nabla^2 u_{ij},$$
$$\frac{dv_{ij}}{dt} = u_{ij} - cv_{ij} + e + \xi_{ij}(t),$$
(5.1)

or in the slow variable $v(t)$

$$\frac{du_{ij}}{dt} = \frac{1}{\epsilon}[u_{ij}(1-u_{ij})(u_{ij}-a) - v_{ij} + d] + D_u\nabla^2 u_{ij},$$
$$\frac{dv_{ij}}{dt} = u_{ij} - cv_{ij} + e + \xi_{ij}(t) + F_{ij}(K,t,\tau).$$
(5.2)

Two different types of the feedback term $F_{ij}(K,t,\tau)$ are investigated, namely local feedback [Eq. (2.8)] and global feedback [Eq. (2.9)]. All simulations presented in this section, are performed using parameter set 1, $e = 0.0$, and $c = 4.6$. Thus, all elements are oscillatory [regime $O1$, cf. Fig. 3.1 (a)]. If feedback is applied, it inserts after $t = 4.0\,t.u.$ of the simulation time. Apart from a short transient, the specific point in time, when the feedback is switched on, has no effect on the presented results. N is either equal to 1 (single element) or equal to 200. Starting with random initial conditions, the net shows globally synchronized oscillations after $t = 4.0\,t.u.$ (before the feedback sets in), if the coupling is strong enough.

5.1.1 Influence of Time-Delayed Feedback on a Single Element

Without feedback ($K = 0.0$), a single FHN element performs autonomous limit cycle oscillations [Figs. 5.1 (a) and 5.1 (b) for $t < 4\,t.u.$]. First, the influence of local feedback in the slow variable $v(t)$ [Eqs. (5.2)] is investigated. Switching on the feedback signal at $t = 4.0\,t.u.$ with $K = 1.0$ and $\tau = 0.5\,t.u.$, the former unstable focus becomes stabilized [Figs. 5.1 (a) and 5.1 (b)]. Only very small oscillations around the fixed point occur [not visible in Figs. 5.1 (a) and 5.1 (b)]. The element rests quasi in its stabilized fixed point. Since the amplitude of the oscillation tends to zero, this effect is called *amplitude death* [71, 72]. If the feeback signal is switched off, the amplitude of the oscillation increases again until the limit cycle is reached. The applied feedback control scheme is non-invasive in that sense that the feedback signal tends to zero [Fig. 5.1 (b)], when the element remains in the stabilized fixed point. In the amplitude death regime, the FHN element is excitable. Applying a small perturbation does not excite the element. Its trajectory runs directly back to the fixed point [Fig. 5.1 (c)]. A perturbation, which drives the element beyond a certain threshold, leads to a large excursion through the phase space, before the trajectory returns to the fixed point [Fig. 5.1 (c)]. In Fig. 5.1 (d), a time series of a single FHN element with feedback, which gets randomly excited by weak additive noise, is shown. The applied feedback ($K = 1.0$ and $\tau = 0.5\,t.u.$) stabilizes the fixed point and the noise provokes the spikes. Such a spiking behavior is typical for excitable neuronal dynamics. Thus, the time-delayed feedback can suppress the oscillation and can induce excitable behavior, which allows for signal transmission.

5.1. OSCILLATORY FITZHUGH-NAGUMO ELEMENTS

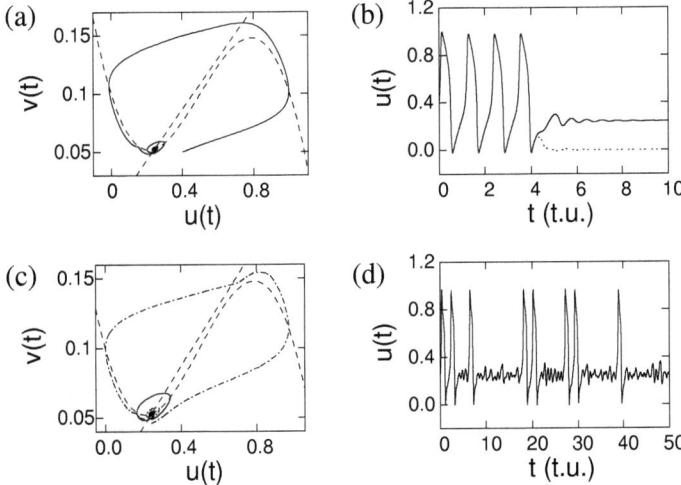

Figure 5.1: *Single FHN element [Eqs. (5.2)]. (a) (—) Trajectory in the phase space with (- - -) nullclines and (b) (—) the corresponding time series. (a), (b) The stabilization of the fixed point, when feedback in the variable $v(t)$ is applied after $t = 4\,t.u.$ (b) ($\cdots$) the feedback signal [Eq. (2.8)]. (c), (d) Excitable behavior in the amplitude death regime. (c) Trajectories for two different initial conditions, (—) below and (—·—) above the excitation threshold. (- - -) Nullclines. (d) (—) Time series when additive noise is applied ($\sigma_{n,e} = 0.005$), a transient of $10\,t.u.$ is cut off. Parameter set 1, $c = 4.6$, $e = 0.0$, $K = 1.0$, $\tau = 0.5\,t.u.$, $g_f = 1.0$, $N = 1$ [48].*

Now the influence of the feedback parameters is studied in detail. The time-average M of $u(t)$ is used as an order parameter to discern the different dynamical regimes (see section 4.3). In Fig. 5.2 (a), the measure M is plotted dependent on the feedback strength K and the delay time τ. If the element performs limit cycle oscillations, the value of M is approximately 0.42 [black region in Fig. 5.2 (a)]. If the element is in the amplitude death regime, the value of M is close to 0.24, the u-coordinate of the fixed point [white region in Fig. 5.2 (a)]. The stabilization of the fixed point is reached for $K > 0.2$ and $0.3\,t.u. < \tau < 0.7\,t.u.$ For the given set of parameters, a linear stability analysis of the model equations without feedback yields a complex conjugated pair of eigenvalues $\lambda = \gamma \pm i\omega = 0.245 \pm i8.75$, where γ denotes the damping rate and ω the intrinsic frequency. Thus, the corresponding intrinsic period of the oscillations in the vicinity of the unstable focus is given by $T_f = \frac{2\pi}{\omega} = 0.718\,t.u.$ Besides this characteristic time scale, the period of the limit cycle $T_{LC} \approx 1.14\,t.u.$ determines the dynamics of the oscillatory FHN element. To reach the amplitude death regime, one has to disturb the limit cycle oscillation and to stabilize the former unstable focus. Applying time-delayed feedback, on the one hand the limit cycle motion is stabilized for $\tau \approx kT_{LC}$ [24], where $k = 0, 1, 2, 3, ...$ is an integer, and

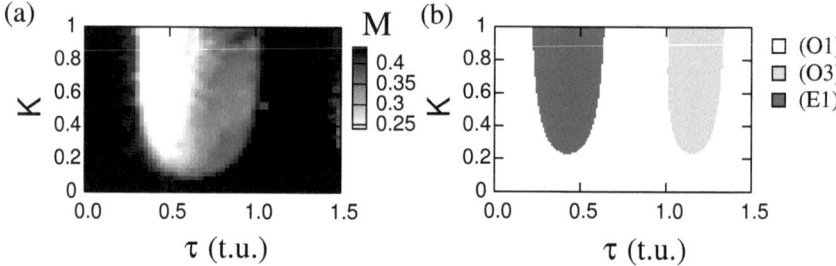

Figure 5.2: (a) The time-average M of $u(t)$ for a single uncoupled FHN element with feedback in $v(t)$ [Eqs. (5.2)] dependent on the feedback parameters K and τ. The white region marks the amplitude death regime, the dark region the oscillatory regime. (b) Result of the linear stability analysis. White region: Unstable focus surrounded by a stable limit cycle. Blue region: Stable focus. Green region: Coexistence of a stable focus and a stable limit cycle. Further parameters: Parameter set 1, $c = 4.6$, $e = 0.0$, $g_f = 1.0$, $N = 1$ [29].

it is disturbed, if τ is not close to kT_{LC}, e.g. for $\tau \approx \frac{1}{2}T_{LC} = 0.57\,t.u.$ On the other hand, the stabilization of an unstable focus is optimally, if the delay time of the feedback is close to the half intrinsic period $T_f/2 \approx 0.36\,t.u.$ [47]. This explains, why the amplitude death regime is found for the interval $0.3\,t.u. < \tau < 0.7\,t.u$, which includes $T_f/2 = 0.36\,t.u.$ and $T_{LC}/2 = 0.57\,t.u.$ The gray areas in Fig. 5.2 (a) (mainly for $0.7\,t.u. < \tau < 1.0\,t.u.$) mark regimes, where the dynamics has very long transients or shows complex oscillations with varying amplitudes.

To validate the numerical simulations, a linear stability analysis of Eqs. (5.2) is performed. Regarding a single element, the linearization of Eqs. (5.2) leads to

$$\dot{\delta u} = \frac{1}{\epsilon}[-3u_{st}^2\delta u + 2(a+1)u_{st}\delta u - a\delta u - \delta v],$$
$$\dot{\delta v} = \delta u - c\delta v + K\delta v(t-\tau) - K\delta v,$$
(5.3)

where the ansatz $x = x_{st} + \delta x$ is used for the variables $u(t)$ and $v(t)$. Thereby x_{st} denotes the stationary solution and δx a small perturbation of this solution. Using the ansatz $\delta x = x_0 \exp(\Lambda t)$ for the temporal evolution of the perturbation, one obtains the following transcendental characteristic equation

$$\Lambda^2 + \nu\Lambda - K\Lambda e^{-\Lambda\tau} - \theta K e^{-\Lambda\tau} + \rho = 0,$$
(5.4)

where the parameters ν, θ, and ρ are given by:

$$\nu = \frac{3}{\epsilon}u_{st}^2 - \frac{2}{\epsilon}(a+1)u_{st} + \frac{a}{\epsilon} + c + K$$
(5.5)

$$\theta = \frac{3}{\epsilon}u_{st}^2 - \frac{2}{\epsilon}(a+1)u_{st} + \frac{a}{\epsilon}$$
(5.6)

$$\rho = \left(\frac{3}{\epsilon}u_{st}^2 - \frac{2}{\epsilon}(a+1)u_{st} + \frac{a}{\epsilon}\right)(c+k) + \frac{1}{\epsilon}.$$
(5.7)

5.1. OSCILLATORY FITZHUGH-NAGUMO ELEMENTS

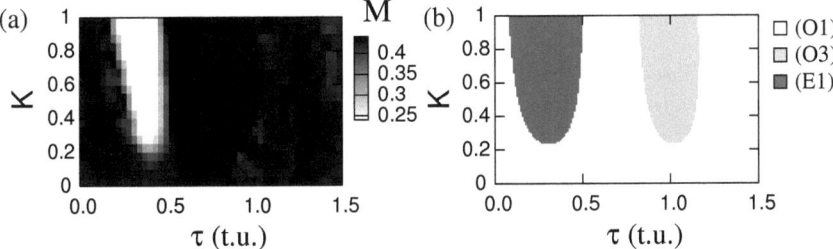

Figure 5.3: (a) The time-average M of $u(t)$ for a single uncoupled FHN element with feedback in $u(t)$ [Eqs. (5.1)] dependent on K and τ. The white region marks the amplitude death regime. (b) Result of the linear stability analysis. White region: Unstable focus surrounded by a stable limit cycle. Blue region: Stable focus. Green region: Coexistence of a stable focus and a stable limit cycle. Further parameters: Parameter set 1, $c = 4.6$, $e = 0.0$, $g_f = 1.0$, $N = 1$.

The transcendental characteristic equation provides an infinite set of eigenvalues Λ, where the eigenvalues Λ with the largest real part determine the temporal evolution of the perturbation. For the given set of parameters, Eq. (5.4) is solved numerically dependent on the feedback parameters K and τ. A two dimensional Newton algorithm is used for various initial values of Λ. Of course, one can never be sure that one has found the eigenvalues with the largest real part, but here only the differentiation $\Lambda \gtrless 0$ is of importance and the result, which is plotted in Fig. 5.2 (b), is convincing. The white region in Fig. 5.2 (b) means that at least one pair of eigenvalues with positive real part exists. The focus is unstable and surrounded by a stable limit cycle (regime $O1$). The element is oscillating [cf. Fig. 5.2 (a)]. In the blue region of Fig. 5.2 (b), no eigenvalue with positive real part exists. Here the focus is stable, which corresponds to the amplitude death regime. Comparing this result with the numerical simulations shown in Fig. 5.2 (a), one discerns that the linear stability analysis predicts very well the amplitude death regime. In the green region, also no eigenvalue with positive real part exists. In this parameter region the stable focus (very small area of attraction) and the stable limit cycle coexist. Because of the initial conditions, the element remains oscillating, and no amplitude death is found in the simulations [Fig. 5.2 (a)]. The coexistence of the two attractors can be explained again by the relevant time scales of the oscillatory element. On the one hand, the focus is stabilized if the delay time is close to an odd multiple of the half of the intrinsic period ($\tau \approx \frac{2k-1}{2}T_f$, where $k = 1, 2, 3, ...$ is an integer) [47]. Thus for $\tau \approx \frac{3}{2}T_f = 1.08\,t.u.$, one expects to find a stable focus, which fits to the result of the linear stability analysis. On the other hand, the limit cycle motion is stable for $\tau \approx T_{LC} = 1.14\,t.u.$ [24], which is confirmed by the numerical simulations [Fig. 5.2 (a)]. For larger values of τ ($1.6\,t.u. < \tau < 1.9\,t.u.$), which is close to $\frac{3}{2}T_{LC} = 1.71\,t.u.$ and $\frac{5}{2}T_f = 1.80\,t.u.$, consequently another region of amplitude death is found.

Regarding large values of the feedback strength ($K > 1$), the amplitude death regime is found till $K \approx 4.1$. For even larger values of K, the fixed point can not be stabilized anymore.

Next the feedback term is introduced in the fast variable $u(t)$ [Eqs. (5.1)]. Dependent on the feedback parameters K and τ, one again finds a region of amplitude death and a region of the coexistence of the stable focus and the stable limit cycle. Generally, all statements done for the system with feedback in the variable $v(t)$, also hold for the case of feedback in the variable $u(t)$. In Fig. 5.3 (a), the measure M is plotted in dependency on the feedback strength K and the delay time τ. The amplitude death regime [white region in Fig. 5.3 (a)] is placed around $\tau \approx \frac{1}{2}T_f$ and not close to kT_{LC} with $k \in \{0, 1\}$. Again the numerical results are confirmed by the result of the linear stability analysis [Fig 5.3 (b)]. Analog to the previous case, the linear stability analysis yields a transcendental characteristic equation, which can be solved numerically. The color coding of Fig 5.3 (b) is the same as of Fig 5.2 (b). Besides the amplitude death regime, the coexistence of the two attractors is found, which is placed around $\tau \approx \frac{3}{2}T_f = 1.08\,t.u.$ (stable focus) and $\tau \approx 1T_{LC} = 1.14\,t.u.$ (stable limit cycle). Again further amplitude death regions exist for larger values of τ. Both the numerical results and the linear stability analysis for feedback in the variable $u(t)$ show that the amplitude death regime is shifted of approximately $0.15\,t.u.$ towards smaller values of τ compared to the case of feedback in $v(t)$. And in contrast to the case of feedback in the variable $v(t)$, in Fig. 5.3 (a) no gray areas exist, i.e. the regime of complex oscillations is not found. Unfortunately, this slight differences could not be explained yet.

5.1.2 Suppression of Global Oscillation in a Net

Feedback in the Variable $v(t)$

Now the influence of the feedback signal on nets of FHN elements is investigated. First feedback in the variable $v(t)$ is considered [Eqs. (5.2)]. In Figs. 5.4 (a)-(c), snapshots of the variable $u_{ij}(t)$ for different consecutive times t show the temporal evolution of the net

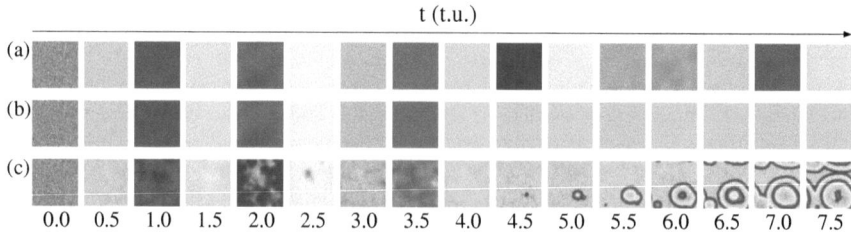

Figure 5.4: *Snapshots of the variable $u_{ij}(t)$ of a net of oscillatory FHN elements [Eqs. (5.2)] for different consecutive times t. Gray scales as in Fig. 3.9. (a) Without feedback and noise: Global oscillation. (b),(c) With local feedback in $v(t)$ ($K = 1.0$, $\tau = 0.5\,t.u.$, $g_f = 0.5$, $\lambda_\mu = 0.0$) that inserts at $t = 4\,t.u.$ (b) Amplitude death ($\sigma_{n,e} = 0.0$). (c) With weak additive noise ($\sigma_{n,e} = 0.03$): Noise-induced pattern formation. Further parameters: Parameter set 1, $c = 4.6$, $e = 0.0$, $N = 200$, $D_u = 50$ [48].*

5.1. OSCILLATORY FITZHUGH-NAGUMO ELEMENTS

dynamics. Without feedback, each element of the net performs limit cycle oscillations. Due to the strong coupling ($D_u = 50$), all elements oscillate synchronously after a short transient [global oscillation, Fig. 5.4 (a)]. If spatially uncorrelated, local feedback ($\lambda_\mu = 0.0$) with appropriately chosen parameter values is applied, all elements remain in the stabilized fixed point [amplitude death, Fig. 5.4 (b)]. The global oscillation is suppressed. In Fig. 5.4 (c), additive noise ($\sigma_{n,e} = 0.03$) is applied in addition to the feedback. The net is in the amplitude death regime, and the noise induces excitation waves, which are supported by the net. The wave fronts propagate through the whole net, which is a signature of excitable behavior [32]. For the investigated parameter range, the amplitude death regime shows always excitable dynamics. For that reason, the terms *amplitude death regime* and *excitable regime* are used synonymously throughout this chapter.

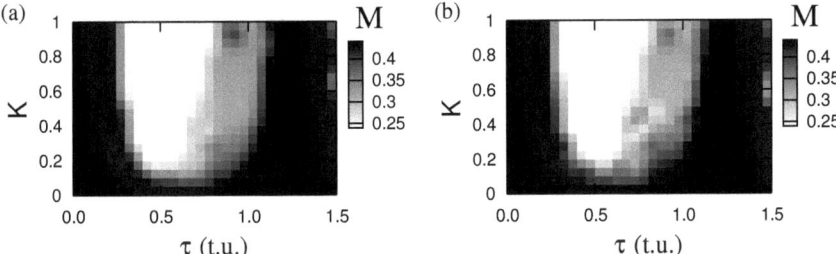

Figure 5.5: *The time-averaged mean field M [Eq. (4.12)] for a net of FHN elements with feedback in $v(t)$ [Eqs. (5.2)] dependent on the feedback parameters K and τ. The white region ($M \approx 0.24$, the value of the fixed point) marks the amplitude death regime. (a) Local feedback [Eq. (2.8)]. (b) Global feedback [Eq. (2.9)]. Further parameters: Parameter set 1, $c = 4.6$, $e = 0.0$, $N = 200$, $D_u = 50$, $g_f = 1.0$, $\lambda_\mu = 0.0$, $\sigma_{n,e} = 0.0$ [48].*

A detailed investigation of the influence of the feedback parameters reveals interesting results. Strongly coupled nets are considered ($D_u = 50$). First all elements get the feedback signal, i.e. $g_f = 1.0$. In Fig 5.5 (a), the time-averaged mean field M [Eq. (4.12)] is plotted dependent on the feedback parameters K and τ for the local feedback. Similar to the results of the single element, the amplitude death regime [white region in Fig 5.5 (a)] is found for $0.3\,t.u. < \tau < 0.7\,t.u.$ and $K \geq 0.2$. For global feedback, the results are very similar [Fig 5.5 (b)]. Due to the strong coupling, all elements are synchronized after a short transient. The time series of the mean field of $v_{ij}(t)$ [here the global feedback is applied in the slow variable $v_{ij}(t)$] is thus very close to the time series of a single element. This statement still holds, when the feedback signal is switched on, because all elements get the feedback signal. For that reason, there is such a little difference between the impact of the local and the global feedback on the network dynamics.

For all further studies presented in this subsection, the delay time is fixed at $\tau = 0.5\,t.u.$, a value, for which the global oscillation of the net is suppressed for $K \gtrsim 0.2$. Next the quota g_f of elements that get the feedback signal is varied. The elements that get the feedback signal are spatially uncorrelated ($\lambda_\mu = 0.0$). The net contains now two different

CHAPTER 5. CONTROL OF OSCILLATORY DYNAMICS

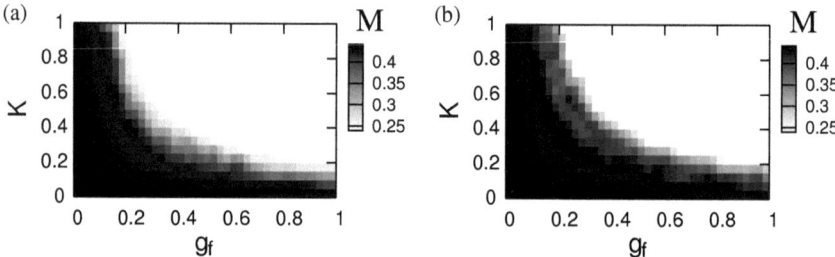

Figure 5.6: *The time-averaged mean field M [Eq. (4.12)] for a net of FHN elements with feedback in $v(t)$ [Eqs. (5.2)] dependent on the feedback parameters K and g_f. (a) Local feedback [Eq. (2.8)]. (b) Global feedback [Eq. (2.9)]. Further parameter: Parameter set 1, $c = 4.6$, $e = 0.0$, $N = 200$, $D_u = 50$, $\tau = 0.5\,t.u.$, $\lambda_\mu = 0.0$, $\sigma_{n,e} = 0.0$ [48].*

kinds of elements, elements with and without the feedback signal. In Fig. 5.6 (a), M is plotted dependent on K and g_f for the local feedback. If K is below a critical value ($K < 0.2$), the amplitude death regime [white region in Fig. 5.6 (a)] is not reached. For $K \approx 0.2$, the whole net remains in the fixed point, if almost all elements get the feedback signal. For larger values of K, it is sufficient to control a smaller quota g_f of elements via the feedback signal to reach the amplitude death regime. If for example K is equal to 1.0, only 20% of all elements have to get the feedback signal to force the whole net to remain in the fixed point. So a small fraction of all elements can determine the dynamics of the whole net. The symmetric structure regarding the influence of the parameters K and g_f is clearly visible. For larger values of the feedback strength K, less elements have to be controlled by the feedback to reach the amplitude death regime and vice versa.

Without coupling, the elements that get the feedback signal ($K > 0.2$) are in the amplitude death regime (excitable elements). Their fixed point is stabilized due to the time-delayed feedback. The other elements are still in the oscillatory regime. With coupling the dynamics of the heterogeneous net depends on the ratio of excitable and oscillatory elements and their spatial distribution, on the excitation threshold of the excitable elements, and on the coupling strength. Controlling a major part of elements (e.g. $g_f = 0.8$) via time-delayed feedback ($K > 0.2$), due to the strong coupling the oscillatory elements, which are uncorrelated and thus well distributed over the whole net, become stabilized fixed points. Reducing the quota of elements that get the feedback signal, only for a larger feedback strength K, the amplitude death regime is found. With increasing feedback strength, the excitation threshold of the controlled elements increases. Thus for larger values of K, less excitable elements (smaller value of g_f) can enforce that the whole net is in the amplitude death regime. At the border between global oscillation and amplitude death, the dynamics is even more complex.

To explain this behavior, snapshots of the variable $u_{ij}(t)$ of the net after $t = 20\,t.u.$ are displayed in Fig. 5.7 dependent on K and g_f for the local feedback. If either K or g_f is below a critical value ($K < 0.1$ and $g_f < 0.1$, respectively) or both parameters are

5.1. OSCILLATORY FITZHUGH-NAGUMO ELEMENTS

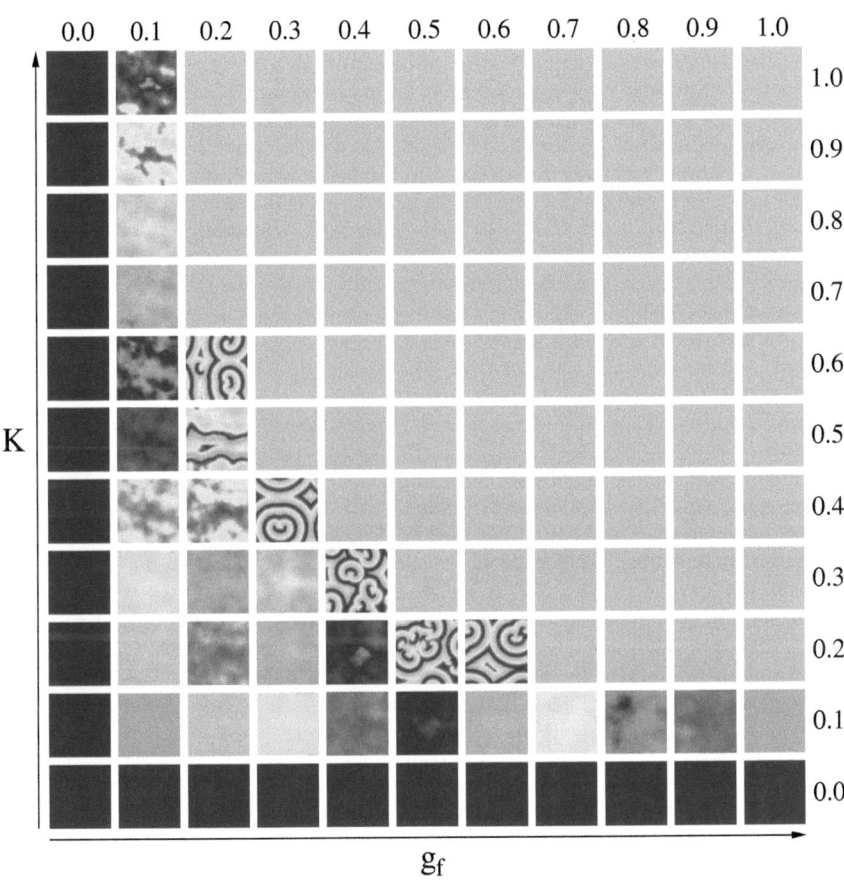

Figure 5.7: *Snapshots of the variable $u_{ij}(t)$ of a net of FHN elements with feedback in $v(t)$ [Eqs. (5.2)] after $t = 20\,t.u.$ dependent on the feedback parameters K and g_f. Local feedback [Eq. (2.8)]. Gray scales as in Fig. 3.9. Further parameters: Parameter set 1, $c = 4.6$, $e = 0.0$, $N = 200$, $D_u = 50$, $\tau = 0.5\,t.u.$, $\lambda_\mu = 0.0$, $\sigma_{n,e} = 0.0$.*

small, the net performs globally synchronized oscillations. For slightly greater values of K and g_f, respectively, patterns, mostly spiral waves, emerge. The patterns are placed along the border of the amplitude death regime and occur independently of the initial conditions, although no noise is applied. Close to the amplitude death regime, the excitable elements ($g_{ij} = 1.0$) can not enforce all oscillatory elements ($g_{ij} = 0.0$) to become stabilized fixed points. Due to the specific mixture of oscillatory and excitable elements and their distribution, a few small clusters of elements remain oscillating. These clusters of oscillating elements excite their neighboring elements and wave fronts spread out over the whole net. Such clusters of oscillating elements, which are placed at the tip of a spiral wave or in the center of a circular wave, are denominated as excitation centers of the waves. For large enough values of K and g_f, the net is in the amplitude death regime, all elements remain in the stabilized fixed point. The spatially homogeneous, temporally constant solution is stable. As mentioned above, the net shows excitable dynamics in the amplitude death regime. So it is possible to excite spiral waves, which are also stable solutions of the net.

Considering global feedback, one qualitatively gets the same result [Fig. 5.6 (b)] as for the local feedback. For a larger feedback strength, the amplitude death regime is already reached by controlling a smaller quota of all elements. If only a fraction of all elements ($g_f < 1$) gets the feedback signal with $K > 0.2$, the net is a mixture of oscillatory and excitable elements. That has a direct impact on the time series of the mean field of $v_{ij}(t)$ and thereby on the global feedback signal. Due to the strong coupling, nevertheless the global oscillation can be suppressed for a large range of the feedback parameters. The border of the amplitude death regime is shifted a little towards greater values of K and g_f, respectively, compared to the result for the local feedback. Here the local feedback is a bit more efficient than the global feedback regarding the suppression of the global oscillation.

So far for all results with $g_f < 1.0$, the selection of the elements that get the feedback signal has been spatially uncorrelated. Regarding for example a medical application, where an external control of a neural tissue would affect not single neurons but clusters of neurons, the spatial correlation is of importance. Consequently, the influence of the feedback control on the global oscillation is studied in dependency on the spatial correlation length λ_μ (see section 2.2) of the controlled elements. Therefore, besides the delay time ($\tau = 0.5\,t.u.$), the quota of elements that get the feedback signal is fixed, namely $g_f = 0.5$. Varying λ_μ means that the cluster size of the controlled elements is changed. As explained in section 2.2, the values of the matrix elements g_{ij} (realization of g_{ij}) are based on a realization of a spatially exponentially correlated Gaussian distributed variable μ_{ij}. The results presented in Fig. 5.8 are the average of ten simulations for different realizations of g_{ij}. In Fig. 5.8 (a), M is plotted dependent on K and λ_μ for the local feedback. For small values of the correlation length λ_μ ($\lambda_\mu < 1.5$), the amplitude death regime [white region in Fig. 5.8 (a)] is reached for $K \gtrsim 0.25$, as in the case $\lambda_\mu = 0.0$ [cf. Fig. 5.6 (a)]. For larger values of λ_μ, the amplitude death regime is found for larger values of the feedback strength K. If $\lambda_\mu > 3.0$, no amplitude death is found anymore. For small λ_μ, the clusters of oscillatory elements ($g_{ij} = 0.0$) are small. Thus due to the coupling, the controlled elements ($g_{ij} = 1.0$) can enforce the oscillatory ones to become stabilized fixed points for $K \gtrsim 0.25$. If the clusters of oscillatory elements are too large ($\lambda_\mu > 3.0$), only the oscillatory elements, which are placed next to controlled elements, are forced to become stabilized fixed points. But some elements in the centers of large clusters of $g_{ij} = 0.0$ remain oscillating. These elements

5.1. OSCILLATORY FITZHUGH-NAGUMO ELEMENTS

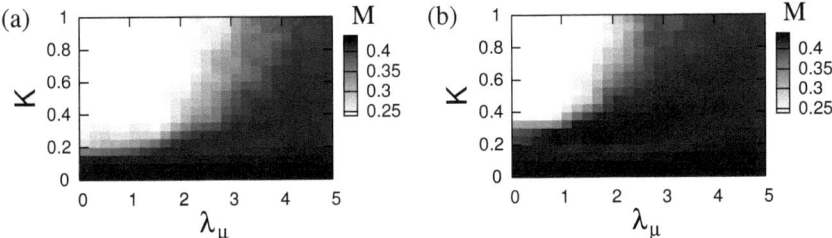

Figure 5.8: *The time-averaged mean field M [Eq. (4.12)] for a net of FHN elements with feedback in $v(t)$ [Eqs. (5.2)] dependent on the feedback strength K and the correlation length λ_μ. Average over ten realizations. (a) Local feedback [Eq. (2.8)]. (b) Global feedback [Eq. (2.9)]. Further parameters: Parameter set 1, $c = 4.6$, $e = 0.0$, $N = 200$, $D_u = 50$, $\tau = 0.5\,t.u.$, $g_f = 0.5$, $\sigma_{n,e} = 0.0$.*

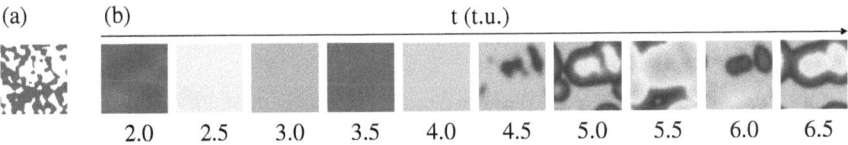

Figure 5.9: *(a) A realization of g_{ij} for $g_f = 0.5$ and $\lambda_\mu = 3.0$. Black denotes $g_{ij} = 1.0$ and white $g_{ij} = 0.0$. (b) Snapshots of the variable $u_{ij}(t)$ of a net of FHN elements with feedback in $v(t)$ [Eqs. (5.2)] for different consecutive times t. The local feedback [Eq. (2.8), $K = 0.5$, $\tau = 0.5\,t.u.$, $g_f = 0.5$, $\lambda_\mu = 3.0$] inserts at $t = 4\,t.u.$ Further parameters: Parameter set 1, $c = 4.6$, $e = 0.0$, $N = 200$, $D_u = 50$, $\sigma_{n,e} = 0.0$.*

act as excitation centers. They excite their neighboring elements and wave fronts travel through the whole net [Fig. 5.9 (b)]. Hence for large correlation lengths λ_μ, the global oscillation is disturbed, because waves travel through the net, but no amplitude death can be realized anymore. In Fig. 5.9 (a), a realization of the matrix g_{ij} is plotted for $\lambda_\mu = 3.0$. Black denotes $g_{ij} = 1.0$, and white $g_{ij} = 0.0$. In Fig. 5.9 (b), the corresponding time series of the net, where the feedback inserts at $t = 4.0\,t.u.$, is plotted. Within the larger clusters without feedback control [upper right corner of Fig. 5.9 (a)], some elements remain oscillating. These elements excite permanently their neighboring elements and wave fronts spread out through the whole net. No amplitude death is found anymore. Thus to stabilize the fixed point of all elements, and to induce excitable dynamics, by controlling only half of the elements, the controlled clusters have to be small and well distributed over the net.

In Fig. 5.8 (b), M is plotted dependent on K and λ_μ for the global feedback. For small values of the correlation length λ_μ ($\lambda_\mu < 1.0$), the amplitude death regime [white region in Fig. 5.8 (b)] is reached for $K \gtrsim 0.35$, consistently to the case $\lambda_\mu = 0.0$ [cf. Fig. 5.6 (b)]. Again, for larger values of λ_μ, the amplitude death regime is found for larger values of the

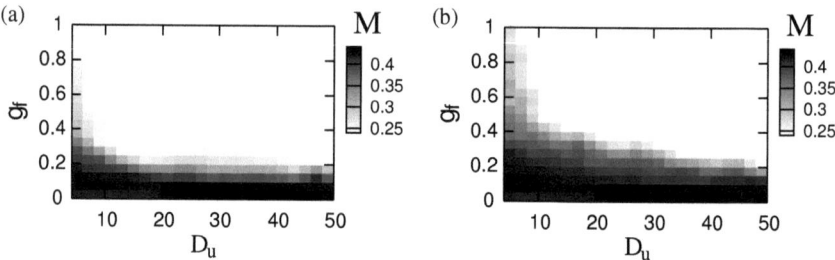

Figure 5.10: *The time-averaged mean field M [Eq. (4.12)] for a net of FHN elements with feedback in v(t) [Eqs. (5.2)] dependent on the feedback parameter g_f and the coupling strength D_u. (a) Local feedback [Eq. (2.8)]. (b) Global feedback [Eq. (2.9)]. Further parameters: Parameter set 1, $c = 4.6$, $e = 0.0$, $N = 200$, $K = 1.0$, $\tau = 0.5\,t.u.$, $\lambda_\mu = 0.0$, $\sigma_{n,e} = 0.0$ [48].*

feedback strength K. If $\lambda_\mu > 2.5$, no amplitude death is found anymore. The explanation for that is the same as for local feedback.

Finally, the influence of the coupling strength D_u on the network dynamics is investigated. Besides the delay time ($\tau = 0.5\,t.u.$), now the feedback strength is fixed ($K = 1.0$). That means that the elements, which get the feedback signal, are in the amplitude death regime. Again spatially uncorrelated feedback ($\lambda_\mu = 0.0$) is applied and the quota g_f of elements that get the feedback signal is varied. In Fig. 5.10 (a), M is plotted dependent on g_f and D_u for the local feedback. For large coupling strengths ($D_u \gtrsim 20$), the transition from the global oscillation to the excitable net dynamics [amplitude death regime, white region in Fig. 5.10 (a)] takes place at $g_f \approx 0.2$ independent of the coupling strength. For smaller coupling strengths, the transition to the amplitude death regime depends on D_u. The smaller the coupling strength D_u is, the more elements have to get the feedback signal (greater value of g_f) to reach the amplitude death regime. In the limit $D_u \to 0$, the collective dynamics gets lost. The elements that get the feedback signal remain in the fixed point, while the others oscillate. For very small coupling strengths, more complicated states may occur, which are not discussed in detail in this thesis. If all elements get the feedback signal with $K = 1.0$ and $\tau = 0.5$, the spatially homogeneous, temporally constant solution is always stable, even for $D_u = 0$, because for local feedback each element remains in its stabilized fixed point. But that is no collective dynamics and the net does not show excitable dynamics (traveling wave fronts).

In Fig. 5.10 (b), the time-averaged mean field M is plotted for the same parameters, but for global feedback. For large coupling strengths ($D_u \gtrsim 35$), the transition from the global oscillation to the amplitude death regime takes place at $g_f \approx 0.22$ nearly independent of the coupling strength. In the limit of very large coupling strengths ($D_u \gtrsim 50$), the difference between the impact of the local and the global feedback is vanishing, regarding the transition from the global oscillation to the excitable net dynamics. For coupling strengths less than $D_u = 35$, the increase of the quota g_f of the elements, which at least have to get the feedback signal to reach the amplitude death regime, is obviously larger compared to the case of local feedback. For small coupling strengths, it takes longer to get a synchronized net dynamics. So the difference between the time series of the mean field of $v_{ij}(t)$ and the time series of a single element is larger. That is the reason for the increasing difference between the impact of the global and the local feedback on the observed transition for weaker coupling. The global feedback is less efficient than the local feedback regarding the suppression of the global oscillation in that sense that more elements have to be controlled by the feedback signal to induce excitable net dynamics.

Feedback in the Variable $u(t)$

Now feedback in the fast variable $u(t)$ is considered [Eqs. (5.1)]. One generally gets the same results as for feedback in the variable $v(t)$. Therefore in this subsection, only the results of the influence of the feedback parameters K, τ, and g_f on the net dynamics for local feedback [Eq. (2.8)] are presented. The coupling strength is again $D_u = 50$ and the selection of the elements that get the feedback signal is done spatially uncorrelated ($\lambda_\mu = 0.0$). In Fig. 5.11 (a), the time-averaged mean field M is plotted in dependency on the feedback strength K and the delay time τ for $g_f = 1.0$. The amplitude death regime found for $K > 0.2$ is placed around $\tau \approx 0.35\,t.u.$ [white region in Fig. 5.11 (a)]. Since all elements get the feedback signal and the coupling is quite strong, the result is very similar to that of a single element [cf. Fig. 5.3 (a)]. For further simulations, the delay time τ is fixed at $\tau = 0.4\,t.u.$, a value, for which the global oscillation is suppressed for $K > 0.2$. Varying K and g_f, the quota of elements that get the feedback signal, the result of M is plotted in Fig. 5.11 (b). One observes again the same qualitative result as for feedback in the variable $v(t)$ [cf. Fig. 5.6 (a)]. For larger values of the feedback strength K, the amplitude death regime is already reached by controlling a smaller quota of all elements. The explanation for the obvious symmetric structure regarding the influence

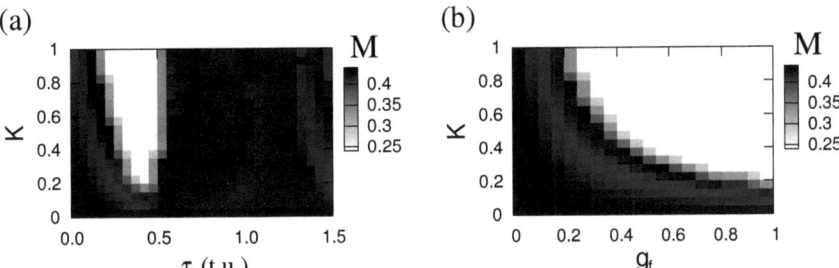

Figure 5.11: *The time-averaged mean field M [Eq. (4.12)] for a net of FHN elements with feedback in $u(t)$ [Eqs. (5.1)]. Local feedback [Eq. (2.8)]. (a) Dependent on K and τ for $g_f = 1.0$. (b) Dependent on K and g_f for $\tau = 0.4\,t.u.$ The white region ($M \approx 0.24$, the value of the fixed point) marks the amplitude death regime. Further parameters: Parameter set 1, $c = 4.6$, $e = 0.0$, $N = 200$, $D_u = 50$, $\lambda_\mu = 0.0$, $\sigma_{n,e} = 0.0$.*

of the feedback parameters K and g_f on the net dynamics, is the same as for the results presented in Fig. 5.6.

Considering global feedback, one obtains even quantitatively almost the same results as for local feedback. Due to the strong coupling, it is obvious that the difference between the impact of global feedback and the impact of local feedback on the net dynamics is marginal [cf. the result for feedback in the variable $v(t)$, Figs. 5.5 (a),(b) and 5.6 (a),(b)]. Studying the influence of the correlation length λ_μ (clustered control) does also not yield qualitative new results compared to the case of feedback in $v(t)$.

5.2 Oscillatory Hodgkin-Huxley Elements

In this section, the influence of time-delayed feedback on oscillatory HH elements is investigated. Similar as for the FHN model, the phenomenon of amplitude death is found for the more complex and realistic HH models. Regarding both, the reduced [Eqs. (3.10)] and the full HH model [Eqs. (3.5)], the feedback term $F_{ij}(K,t,\tau)$ is either introduced in the gating variable $n(t)$ or in the potential variable $V(t)$. Here only local feedback [Eq. (2.8)] is considered. The results for global feedback [Eq. (2.9)] are almost the same. The parameters are given in Eq. (3.7), whereas $I = 9.0\frac{\mu A}{cm^2}$ for the reduced HH model and $I = 10.0\frac{\mu A}{cm^2}$ for the full HH model. Thus, all elements are in the oscillatory regime [cf. Figs. 3.6 (a) and 3.6 (b)]. N is either equal to 1 (single element) or equal to 200. The feedback inserts after $t = 40.0\,ms$ (accords approximately with the duration of three oscillations) of the simulation time. Due to the strong coupling ($D_V = 50$), the net shows global oscillation, before the feedback sets in. To detect the amplitude death regime, the relative rest time T_r [Eq. (4.9)] is used as order parameter throughout this section.

5.2.1 Influence of Time-Delayed Feedback on a Single Element

First, the influence of the feedback on the reduced HH model is investigated. Without feedback, the single element performs autonomous limit cycle oscillations. Applying feedback with appropriately chosen parameter values, it is possible to stabilize the former unstable fixed point. The amplitude of the oscillation tends to zero. In Fig. 5.12 (a), the relative rest time T_r is plotted dependent on K and τ for feedback in the variable $n(t)$. The amplitude death regime is found for $3.7\,ms < \tau < 7.5\,ms$ and $0.05 < K < 0.65$ [white region in Fig. 5.12 (a)]. Applying feedback in the potential variable $V(t)$, the amplitude death regime is also found [white region in Fig. 5.12 (b)], but only for a quite narrow parameter region of τ.

Regarding the full HH model, the phenomenon of amplitude death can be observed for a quite large parameter region of K and τ for both, feedback in $n(t)$ [Fig. 5.13 (a)] and feedback in $V(t)$ [Fig. 5.13 (b)]. Generally, the impact of time-delayed feedback on the dynamics of a HH element (reduced or full model) is quite complex. And it is difficult to explain, why the amplitude death regions are found for such different values of τ and K. Both feedback in $n(t)$ and feedback in $V(t)$ strongly affects the oscillation period, which is about $T_{LC_{full}} \approx 15\,ms$ for the full model and about $T_{LC_{red}} \approx 12.5\,ms$ for the reduced model without feedback. Besides the limit cycle period, the second important time scale is

5.2. OSCILLATORY HODGKIN-HUXLEY ELEMENTS

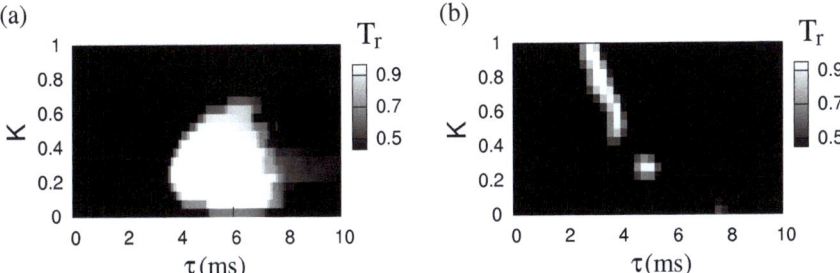

Figure 5.12: *The relative rest time T_r [Eq. (4.9)] for a single HH element [reduced model, Eqs. (3.10)] dependent on K and τ for local feedback [Eq. (2.8)]. The white region marks the amplitude death regime. (a) Feedback in the gating variable $n(t)$. (b) Feedback in the potential variable $V(t)$. Further parameters: Parameters given by Eq. (3.7), $I = 9.0\frac{\mu A}{cm^2}$, $N = 1$.*

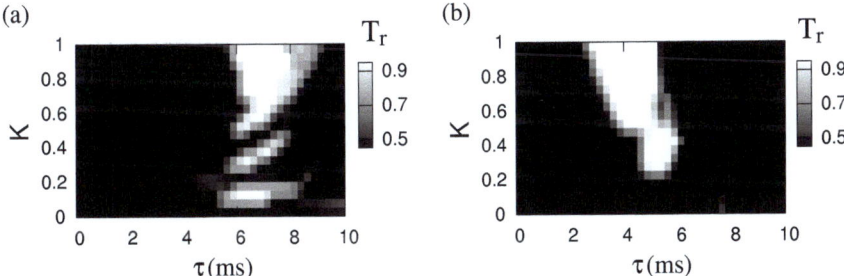

Figure 5.13: *The relative rest time T_r [Eq. (4.9)] for a single HH element [full model, Eqs. (3.5)] dependent on K and τ for local feedback [Eq. (2.8)]. The white region marks the amplitude death regime. (a) Feedback in the gating variable $n(t)$. (b) Feedback in the potential variable $V(t)$. Further parameters: Parameters given by Eq. (3.7), $I = 10.0\frac{\mu A}{cm^2}$, $N = 1$.*

the period of the oscillations in the vicinity of the unstable focus. The half of this period is about $T_{f_{full}}/2 \approx 5.3\,ms$ for the full model and about $T_{f_{red}}/2 \approx 4.8\,ms$ for the reduced model. At least, the amplitude death regions of a single HH element are found again for values of the delay time, which are close to $T_f/2$.

Generally, one can state that time-delayed feedback with appropriately chosen parameter values can suppress the limit cycle oscillation of a HH element. For both the reduced and the full model, the former unstable fixed point can be stabilized. In the amplitude death regime, weak additive noise randomly provokes spikes. Thus, as for the FHN model, the HH elements show excitable behavior in the amplitude death regime.

5.2.2 Suppression of Global Oscillation in a Net

Now the influence of the feedback parameters K, τ, and g_f on the dynamics of oscillatory nets of HH elements is investigated. Throughout this section, the selection of elements that get the feedback signal is done spatially uncorrelated ($\lambda_\mu = 0.0$). First a net of reduced HH elements is studied. In Figs. 5.14 (a) and 5.14 (b), the results for feedback in the gating variable $n(t)$ are displayed. If all elements get the feedback signal ($g_f = 1.0$), the amplitude death regime [white region in Fig. 5.14 (a)] is placed around $\tau \approx 6\,ms$ for $0.05 < K < 0.65$. In the amplitude death regime, all elements remain in the stabilized

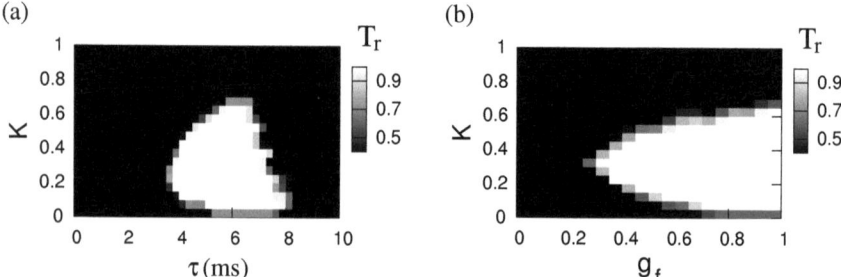

Figure 5.14: *The relative rest time T_r [Eq. (4.9)] for a net of HH elements [reduced model, Eqs. (3.13)] for local feedback in the gating variable $n(t)$. The white region marks the amplitude death regime. (a) Dependent on K and τ for $g_f = 1.0$. (b) Dependent on K and g_f for $\tau = 6.0\,ms$. Further parameters: Parameters given by Eq. (3.7), $I = 9.0\frac{\mu A}{cm^2}$, $N = 200$, $D_V = 50$, $\lambda_\mu = 0.0$.*

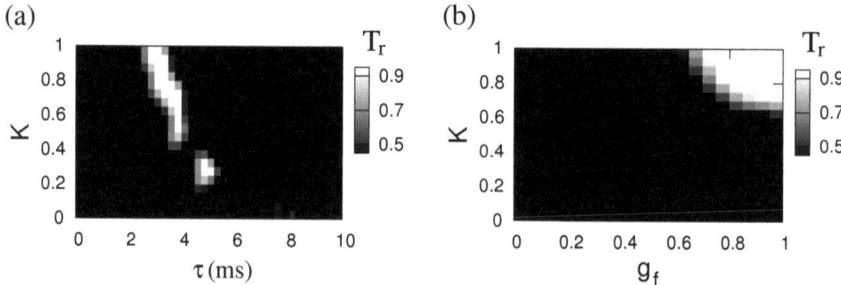

Figure 5.15: *The relative rest time T_r [Eq. (4.9)] for a net of HH elements [reduced model, Eqs. (3.13)] for local feedback in the potential variable $V(t)$. The white region marks the amplitude death regime. (a) Dependent on K and τ for $g_f = 1.0$. (b) Dependent on K and g_f for $\tau = 3.0\,ms$. Further parameters: Parameters given by Eq. (3.7), $I = 9.0\frac{\mu A}{cm^2}$, $N = 200$, $D_V = 50$, $\lambda_\mu = 0.0$.*

5.2. OSCILLATORY HODGKIN-HUXLEY ELEMENTS

fixed point, the global oscillation is suppressed. Since all elements get the feedback signal and the coupling is quite strong, the result again accords with the result of a single element [cf. Fig. 5.12 (a)].

In Fig. 5.14 (b), the relative rest time T_r is plotted dependent on the feedback strength K and g_f, the quota of elements that get the feedback signal. The delay time τ is fixed at $\tau = 6\,ms$, a value, for which the global oscillation is suppressed for $0.05 < K < 0.65$. The white region marks the amplitude death regime. If almost all elements get the feedback signal, the amplitude death regime is reached for $0.05 < K < 0.65$, consistently to the result presented in Fig. 5.14 (a). Increasing K from 0.05 up to 0.35, less and less elements have to get the feedback signal to ensure that the whole net remains in the stabilized fixed point. The explanation therefore is the same as for Fig. 5.6 (a). Then for larger values of K ($0.35 < K < 0.65$), again more and more elements have to be controlled via the feedback signal to suppress the global oscillation. As stated in the explanation of Fig. 5.6 (a), the excitation threshold of the controlled elements, which influences the net dynamics, depends on the feedback strength. For $0.35 < K < 0.65$, one observes that the larger the value of K is, the smaller perturbations are again sufficient to excite the controlled elements (smaller excitation threshold). Thus more and more elements have to be controlled via the feedback signal to reach the amplitude death regime. For an intermediate value of K [$K \approx 0.35$, Fig. 5.14 (b)], the fixed point is optimally stabilized. Here, it is sufficient to control about 30% of the elements to ensure that all elements remain in the stabilized fixed point.

In Figs. 5.15 (a) and 5.15 (b), the results for feedback in the potential variable $V(t)$ are displayed. If all elements get the feedback signal [$g_f = 1.0$, Fig. 5.15 (a)], the amplitude death regime is only found for a narrow parameter region of τ, as for the single element [cf. Fig. 5.12 (b)]. To study the influence of the quota of elements that get the feedback signal on the net dynamics, the delay time τ is fixed at $\tau = 3.0\,ms$. In Fig. 5.15 (b), T_r is plotted dependent on K and g_f. If almost all elements get the feedback signal, the border of amplitude death regime is reached for $K \approx 0.7$. For larger values of K, it is sufficient to control less elements to reach the amplitude death regime. The result is qualitatively the same as for the FHN model [cf. Fig. 5.6 (a) and Fig. 5.11 (b)]. The explanation is given in the corresponding section (section 5.1.2). For another value of τ, e.g. $\tau = 4.8\,ms$, the result regarding the influence of the feedback parameters K and g_f is qualitatively the same as for the case of feedback in $n(t)$ [cf. Fig. 5.14 (b)]. Of course, the amplitude death regime is much smaller and only found for large values of g_f.

Next nets of HH elements obeying the full model equations [Eqs. (3.12)] are studied. Again, one finds qualitatively similar results as for the reduced HH model and the FHN model. For that reason, here only the results considering feedback in the potential variable $V(t)$ are presented [Figs. 5.16 (a) and 5.16 (b)].

If all elements get the feedback signal [$g_f = 1.0$, Fig. 5.16 (a)], the amplitude death regime is placed around $\tau = 4.5\,ms$. Again, the net dynamics accord with the dynamics of a single element [cf. Fig. 5.13 (b)]. In Fig. 5.16 (b), the influence of g_f and K on the net dynamics is displayed for an intermediate value of τ ($\tau = 4.5\,ms$). Again for larger values of K, it is sufficient to control less elements via the feedback signal to reach the amplitude death regime and vice versa [Fig. 5.16 (b)]. The reason for this symmetric structure regarding the impact of the feedback parameters K and g_f is the same as for the

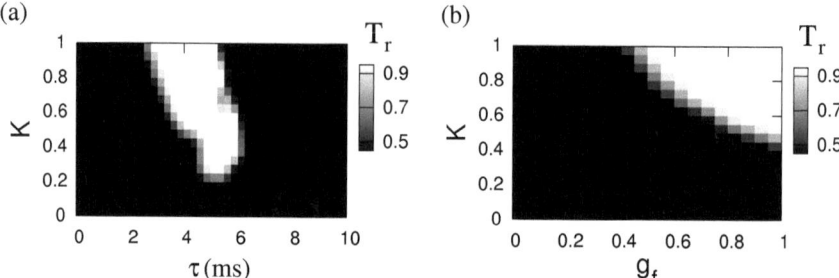

Figure 5.16: *The relative rest time T_r [Eq. (4.9)] for a net of HH elements [full model, Eqs. (3.12)] for local feedback in the gating variable $V(t)$. The white region marks the amplitude death regime. (a) Dependent on K and τ for $g_f = 1.0$. (b) Dependent on K and g_f for $\tau = 4.5\,ms$. Further parameters: Parameters given by Eq. (3.7), $I = 10.0\frac{\mu A}{cm^2}$, $N = 200$, $D_V = 50$, $\lambda_\mu = 0.0$.*

results presented in Figs. 5.6 (a), 5.11 (b), and 5.15 (b). Considering global feedback no qualitatively different results occur [cf. section 5.1.2].

Reducing the coupling strength to $D_V = 10$, one finds even quantitatively the same results. For a coupling strength of $D_V = 1$, one still finds the amplitude death regime, but only for larger values of g_f. Similar as for the FHN model, for small coupling strengths, more elements have to be controlled via the feedback signal to reach the amplitude death regime.

Summarizing, the results presented in this chapter show that time-delayed feedback control provides an efficient method to suppress oscillations and to induce excitable behavior in neural model systems. The amplitude death regime is found for single elements and nets of FHN and HH (full and reduced model) elements, respectively. Regarding nets, it is sufficient to control only a small quota of all elements to reach the amplitude death regime, if the controlled elements are nearly uncorrelated. If the distribution of the controlled elements is highly correlated, no amplitude death can be realized anymore.

Chapter 6

Delay-Sustained Pattern Formation in Subexcitable Media

A number of investigations focus on the dynamics of subexcitable and excitable media. Whereas in subexcitable media excitation waves die out, the typical feature of excitable media is that wave fronts can propagate through the whole system. This excitable behavior allows signal transmission through media, being crucial for the functionality of many physical, chemical, biological and physiological systems, e.g., the pulse propagation in neural tissues.

It is well known that noise can have a constructive influence on the dynamics of subexcitable systems [13]. The existence of noise sustained waves has been confirmed experimentally in slices of hippocampal astrocytes [73]. Further it was shown that noise favors the emergence of spiral waves in a subexcitable Belousov-Zhabotinsky reaction [74]. Another example is the phenomenon of spatiotemporal stochastic resonance (STSR), where the most coherent patterns are found for intermediate noise strengths [32, 33]. Similar to noise, variability can induce pattern formation in subexcitable media [17], where the patterns are most coherent for intermediate variability strengths (variability-induced STSR).

In recent years, besides the influence of stochastic forces on nonlinear media, the control of spatiotemporal dynamics has become a topic of great interest. Studying the occurrence of migraine, one has experienced that excitation waves, which spread over the cortex, spark off the attack of migraine [75, 76, 77]. Thus, it was supposed to use time-delayed feedback to suppress the propagation of the excitations in the cortex. Recently, the Pyragas control scheme has been used to suppress pulse propagation in a chain of excitable FHN elements [25]. In another investigation, a feedback control force is used to stabilize spiral wave dynamics [78]. For many applications, it is important to be able to control pattern forming processes and signal transmission in a desired manner.

In this chapter, the influence of time-delayed feedback on pattern formation in subexcitable media is studied. It is shown that time-delayed feedback can sustain pattern formation [79]. Besides the propagation of wave fronts induced by special initial conditions, noise- and variability-induced patterns under the influence of time-delayed feedback are investigated. Throughout this chapter, only diffusively coupled nets [Eq. (3.15)] with local feedback [Eq. (2.8)] are considered.

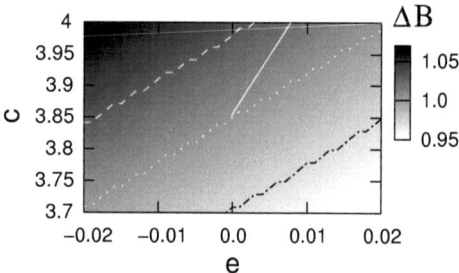

Figure 6.1: ΔB [Eq. (4.19)] dependent on c and e for a single FHN element [Eqs. (3.1)] without feedback. $(-\cdot-)$ $\Delta B = 0.97$, $(\cdots)$ $\Delta B = 1.0$, $(---)$ $\Delta B = 1.03$, The white solid line marks the effective parameter change (for details see section 6.1.1). Further parameters: Parameter set 1, $N = 1$, $\sigma_{n,e} = 0.0$, $\sigma_{v,e} = 0.0$ [79].

6.1 Subexcitable Net of FitzHugh-Nagumo Elements

Throughout this section, the influence of time-delayed feedback on pattern formation in subexcitable nets of FHN elements is investigated. The model equations, where only feedback in the variable $v(t)$ is studied, read

$$\frac{du_{ij}}{dt} = \frac{1}{\epsilon}[u_{ij}(1-u_{ij})(u_{ij}-a) - v_{ij} + d] + D_u \nabla^2 u_{ij},$$
$$\frac{dv_{ij}}{dt} = u_{ij} - cv_{ij} + e_{ij} + \xi_{ij}(t) + F_{ij}(K,t,\tau). \quad (6.1)$$

Applying feedback in the variable $u(t)$, one qualitatively yields the same results. The multiplicative stochastic terms are not considered throughout this section, whereas the additive stochastic terms are used to excite patterns. For all simulations throughout this section, parameter set 1 is used.

Studying first a net of FHN elements without noise, variability, and feedback, whose elements are in the regime $E1$, the net can show two different dynamical behaviors. A wave front induced by special initial conditions can grow and propagate through the whole net (excitable net) or it can shrink and die out (subexcitable net, cf. section 3.3). To gain a better understanding of excitable and subexcitable net dynamics, first an excitation spike of a single element is investigated for varying parameter values of c and e. The duration of the whole spike is composed mainly of the duration of the excitation $B(c,e)$ and the duration of the refractory period $R(c,e)$ (Fig. 4.1). In Fig. 6.1, the normalized time span of an excitation ΔB [Eq. (4.19)] is plotted dependent on the parameters c and e. ΔB increases with increasing values of c and decreasing values of e, whereas the normalized duration of the refractory period ΔR [Eq. (4.20)] does not change significantly with the parameters c and e. Regarding now the dynamics of a net, an excitation wave spreads out, if the elements at the edge of the wave front can excite their neighboring elements. To excite a neighboring element, the duration $B(c,e)$ of the excitation (Fig. 6.1)

6.1. SUBEXCITABLE NET OF FITZHUGH-NAGUMO ELEMENTS

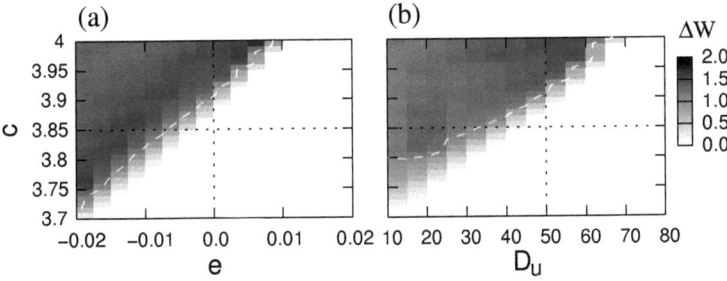

Figure 6.2: ΔW [Eq. (4.21)] for wave fronts induced by special initial conditions in a net of FHN elements [Eqs. 6.1] without feedback. (a) Dependent on c and e for $D_u = 50$. (b) Dependent on c and D_u for $e = 0.0$. ($---$) $\Delta W = 1.0$ marks the border between the subexcitable regime (white area) and the excitable regime (gray area). ($\cdots$) mark the parameter values chosen for all further simulations. Further parameters: Parameter set 1, $N = 100$, $\sigma_{n,e} = 0.0$, $\sigma_{v,e} = 0.0$ [79].

and the coupling strength between the elements play a crucial role. To discern whether the net shows excitable or subexcitable dynamics, the measure ΔW [Eq. (4.21)] is used. Therefore, the temporal evolution of a wave front induced by special initial conditions is studied. Simulations of the net are performed for different parameter values of c, e and D_u. The results are plotted in Fig. 6.2. In both panels, the white dashed line ($\Delta W = 1.0$) marks the border between the subexcitable (white area) and the excitable regime (dark gray area). The dynamics of the net depends on the values of c and e, and on the coupling strength. The dotted lines mark the parameter values chosen for all further simulations throughout this chapter ($c = 3.85$, $e = 0.0$, $D_u = 50$). For these values, the net is in the subexcitable regime.

6.1.1 Time-Delayed Feedback Control of Wave Fronts Induced by Special Initial Conditions

To understand the impact of time-delayed feedback on the propagation of wave fronts through a net of FHN elements, it is essential to study first the influence of time-delayed feedback on the excitation spike of a single element. Both the duration $B(K, \tau)$ of the excitation and the duration $R(K, \tau)$ of the refractory period are elongated due to the feedback (Fig. 6.3). In Fig. 6.4, the change of the excitation spike is quantified. Fig. 6.4 (a) shows the relative change of the duration of the excitation ΔB [Eq. (4.19)]. One discerns that ΔB increases with increasing parameter values of K and τ. When the element is driven from its fixed point beyond the excitation threshold, the delayed state $v(t - \tau)$ is still equal to $v_{st} = 0.052$, the v-coordinate of the fixed point. So at the beginning of the excitation spike, one can replace the feedback term F_{ij} in the second differential equation of Eqs. (6.1) by introducing the effective parameters $c_{tdf} = c + K$ and $e_{tdf} = e + Kv_{st}$ ($c = 3.85$, $e = 0.0$). With an increasing value of K, the parameters c and e are effectively

50 CHAPTER 6. DELAY-SUSTAINED PATTERN FORMATION

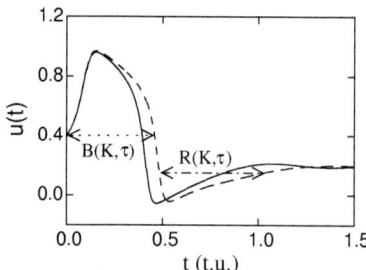

Figure 6.3: *Time series of an excitation spike of a single uncoupled FHN element with feedback in $v(t)$ [Eqs. (6.1); cf. Fig. 4.1 (a)]. (—) Without feedback ($K = 0.0$). (– – –) With feedback ($K = 1.0$, $\tau = 0.3\,t.u.$). Further parameters: Parameter set 1, $c = 3.85$, $e = 0.0$, $g_f = 1.0$, $N = 1$, $\sigma_{n,e} = 0.0$, $\sigma_{v,e} = 0.0$.*

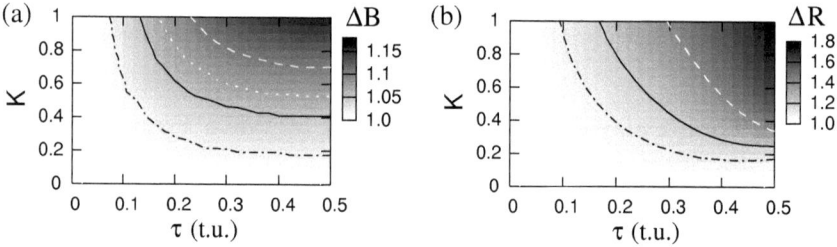

Figure 6.4: *(a) ΔB [Eq. (4.19)] and (b) ΔR [Eq. (4.20)] for a single uncoupled FHN element with feedback in $v(t)$ [Eqs. (6.1)] dependent on the feedback parameters K and τ. (a) (–·–) $\Delta B = 1.02$, (—) $\Delta B = 1.05$, (···) $\Delta B = 1.07$, (– – –) $\Delta B = 1.1$. (b) (–·–) $\Delta R = 1.1$, (—) $\Delta R = 1.2$, (– – –) $\Delta R = 1.4$. Further parameters: Parameter set 1, $c = 3.85$, $e = 0.0$, $g_f = 1.0$, $N = 1$, $\sigma_{n,e} = 0.0$, $\sigma_{v,e} = 0.0$ [79].*

6.1. SUBEXCITABLE NET OF FITZHUGH-NAGUMO ELEMENTS

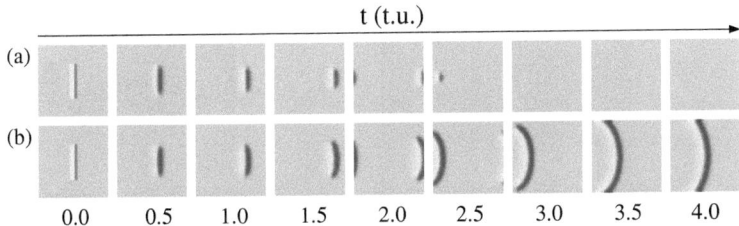

Figure 6.5: *Snapshots of the variable $u_{ij}(t)$ of a net of FHN elements [Eqs. (6.1)] for different consecutive times t. (a) Without feedback: Subexcitable behavior. (b) With local feedback in $v(t)$ ($K = 1.0$, $\tau = 0.3\,t.u.$, $g_f = 1.0$, $\lambda_\mu = 0.0$): Excitable behavior. Gray scales as in Fig. 3.9. Wave fronts induced by special initial conditions. Further parameters: Parameter set 1, $c = 3.85$, $e = 0.0$, $N = 100$, $D_u = 50$, $\sigma_{n,e} = 0.0$, $\sigma_{v,e} = 0.0$.*

shifted to larger values (white solid line in Fig. 6.1), leading to an increase of the duration of the excitation. Regarding the whole spike, the influence of the time-delayed feedback is more complex. Besides the duration of the excitation, the duration of the refractory period is strongly elongated due to the feedback [Fig. 6.4 (b)].

Regarding now a net, the propagation of a wave front induced by special initial conditions is studied under the influence of time-delayed feedback. Throughout this subsection, neither noise nor variability is applied ($\sigma_{n,e} = 0.0$, $\sigma_{v,e} = 0.0$). Without feedback, the wave front dies out after a short propagation length [Fig. 6.5 (a)], because of the subexcitability of the net. Applying time-delayed feedback with appropriately chosen parameter values, the propagation of the wave front is sustained [Fig. 6.5 (b)]. Due to the feedback, which elongates the duration of the excitation, the excited elements are able to excite their neighboring elements and the wave front grows and propagates through the whole net, which is a signature of excitable behavior. Hence, due to the time-delayed feedback, signal transmission through the whole net is possible, which is an important feature of neuronal networks.

To analyse the impact of the feedback on the propagation of a wave front induced by special initial conditions in detail, the measure ΔW [Eq. (4.21)] is used. Fig. 6.6 (a) shows ΔW dependent on K and τ, when all elements get the feedback signal ($g_f = 1.0$, $\lambda_\mu = 0.0$). With increasing parameter values of K and τ, an increase of ΔW is observed. For large enough values for K and τ, the wave front starts to grow. The dashed line ($\Delta W = 1.0$) marks the border between the subexcitable (white region) and the excitable regime (dark gray region). As shown in Fig. 6.4 (a), the feedback signal elongates the duration of the excitation of each element. If the duration of the excitation is large enough, the elements at the edge of the wave front can excite there neighboring elements and the wave front grows and spreads out. In this way, the time-delayed feedback sustains the propagation of wave fronts in the subexcitable net. For large values of τ ($\tau > 0.3\,t.u.$), the transition to the excitable net behavior takes place at $K = 0.35$ independent of τ [see Fig. 6.6 (a)]. This result is confirmed by further simulations up to $\tau = 1.5\,t.u.$

In Fig. 6.6 (b), ΔW is shown dependent on K and g_f for $\tau = 0.3\,t.u.$ The elements

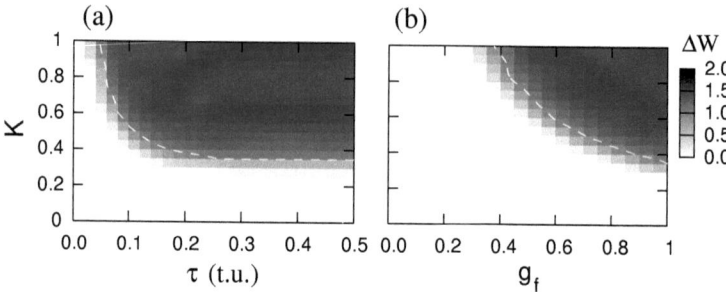

Figure 6.6: ΔW [Eq. (4.21)] for wave fronts in a net of FHN elements with feedback in $v(t)$ [Eqs. 6.1]. (a) Dependent on K and τ for $g_f = 1.0$. (b) Dependent on K and g_f for $\tau = 0.3\,t.u.$ (– – –) $\Delta W = 1.0$ marks the border between the subexcitable regime (white region) and the excitable regime (dark gray region). Initial conditions as in Fig. 6.5. Further parameters: Parameter set 1, $c = 3.85$, $e = 0.0$, $N = 100$, $D_u = 50$, $\lambda_\mu = 0.0$, $\sigma_{n,e} = 0.0$, $\sigma_{v,e} = 0.0$ [79].

that get the feedback signal are spatially uncorrelated ($\lambda_\mu = 0.0$). Again the dashed line ($\Delta W = 1.0$) marks the border between the subexcitable and the excitable regime. For $K \approx 0.4$, the net shows excitable behavior, if almost all elements get the feedback signal. For larger values of K, it is sufficient to control a smaller quota g_f of all elements to reach the excitable regime. If K is equal to 1, only 40% of all elements have to be controlled to sustain the propagation of a wave front induced by special initial conditions. For $g_f < 1.0$, the net contains two different kinds of elements, elements that do not sustain the propagation of a wave front ($g_{ij} = 0.0$) and elements, whose duration of the excitation is elongated due to the feedback ($g_{ij} = 1.0$). Whether the propagation of a wave front is sustained, depends on the number of elements that get the feedback signal and on the duration of the excitation of these elements. An increase of the feedback strength K results in an increase of ΔB [Fig. 6.4 (a)]. Thus, the duration of the excitation of the elements that get the feedback signal is enlarged. As larger the duration of the excitation of some elements at the edge of a wave front, as less elements have to be controlled via the feedback signal to ensure the excitation of the neighboring elements. Consequently, for larger values of K, it is sufficient to control a smaller quota g_f of all elements to sustain the propagation of an excitation wave.

Now, the influence of clustered control, where half of the elements get the feedback signal ($g_f = 0.5$), is studied. The feedback strength K and the delay time τ are chosen to be $K = 0.6$ and $\tau = 0.3\,t.u.$, respectively. For this set of feedback parameters, the net still shows subexcitable behavior [see Fig. 6.6 (b)]. A practical measure for the excitability of a net is the life time of a front. For a net of FHN elements, the life time T_L of a wave front induced by special initial conditions is defined as the largest time, for which $u_{ij}(t) > 0.4$ is found at least for one of the $N \times N$ elements. In Fig. 6.7, T_L is plotted dependent on the correlation length λ_μ of the controlled elements (see section 2.2). The displayed result is

6.1. SUBEXCITABLE NET OF FITZHUGH-NAGUMO ELEMENTS

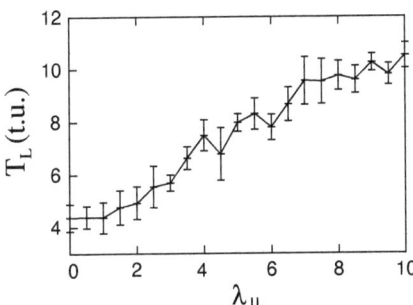

Figure 6.7: *The life time T_L of a wave front in a net of FHN elements with feedback in $v(t)$ [Eqs. (6.1)] dependent on the correlation length λ_μ. Initial conditions as in Fig. 6.5. Further parameters: Parameter set 1, $c = 3.85$, $e = 0.0$, $N = 100$, $D_u = 50$, $K = 0.6$, $\tau = 0.3\,t.u.$, $g_f = 0.5$, $\sigma_{n,e} = 0.0$, $\sigma_{v,e} = 0.0$.*

the average over 100 realizations. The results of the single simulations vary quite strongly, because the life time of a wave front crucially depends on the location and distribution of the randomly created clusters, which are controlled via the feedback. But nevertheless, the probability that a wave front survives the time T_L is strongly influenced by the value of λ_μ. At small values of λ_μ, the averaged life time of the wave front takes its minimum value of $T_L \approx 4.5\,t.u.$ For $\lambda_\mu < 2.0$, the averaged cluster size is small compared to the extension of the excitation wave. So no influence of the correlation length on the life time of the wave front is visible. For larger values of λ_μ, the probability that a wave front survives a longer time increases considerably. A larger value of λ_μ denotes larger clusters of elements that get the feedback signal (Fig. 2.2). Within the controlled clusters, the wave front grows and spreads out, whereas outside of these clusters the wave front shrinks. If the cluster size exceeds the extension of the excitation wave ($\lambda_\mu \gtrsim 2$), the wave front can grow within the controlled clusters, and in average the life time of the excitation wave is increased.

6.1.2 Time-Delayed Feedback Control of Noise-Induced Pattern Formation

Now the influence of the feedback signal on noise-induced pattern formation in the subexcitable net is studied. All simulations are started with random initial conditions, the additive noise strength is fixed at $\sigma_{n,e} = 0.1$, and no variability is considered ($\sigma_{v,e} = 0.0$). Additive noise may excite the elements and can induce wave fronts [17]. Because of the subexcitability of the net, the noise-induced waves die out after a short propagation length [Fig. 6.8 (a)]. Applying time-delayed feedback with appropriately chosen parameter values (e.g. $K = 1.0$, $\tau = 0.3\,t.u.$, $g_f = 1.0$, $\lambda_\mu = 0.0$) the propagation of noise-induced waves is sustained [Fig. 6.8 (b)]. The explanation is the same as for the delay-sustained wave fronts, which are induced by special initial conditions [cf. subsection 6.1.1]. Due to the feedback, which elongates the duration of the excitation, the excited elements are able to excite their neighboring elements and the noise-induced waves grow and spread out through the whole net. The net shows excitable behavior.

To quantify the influence of the time-delayed feedback on the noise-induced patterns, the spatial cross correlation S [Eq. (4.15)] and the mutual information I [Eq. (4.16)] are used. In Fig. 6.9 (a), the spatial cross correlation S of the noise-induced patterns is plotted dependent on the feedback parameters K and τ for $g_f = 1.0$. For small values of K ($K < 0.3$), the noise-induced wave fronts die out very quickly, and thus the spatial cross correlation S is close to zero. The same is valid for small values of τ. For $\tau \geq 0.1\,t.u.$, the coherence of the patterns increases with increasing values of K. Because of the elongated duration of the excitation, the probability that noise-induced wave fronts can spread out through the whole net is increased. If $K \geq 0.6$, coherent pattern formation is sustained for a large range of τ-values, resulting in a large value of S. The dependency of S on the delay time τ is more complex and thus explicitly discussed for the case $K = 1.0$ [Fig. 6.9 (b)]. Increasing the value of τ leads to an elongation of the duration $B(K,\tau)$ of the excitation, thus the wave fronts grow and pattern formation in the net is sustained, resulting in an increase of S. For values of $\tau > 0.25$, the coherence of the patterns slowly decreases. Besides an increase of ΔB [Fig. 6.4 (a)], the feedback leads to an elongation of the refractory period $R(K,\tau)$ [$\Delta R > 1$, Fig. 6.4 (b)]. So for large values of τ, the propagation of waves is still sustained, but the elements remain longer in the refractory period after an excitation wave has passed. The elongation of the refractory period causes that less wave fronts can propagate through the net in a certain time interval. Consequently, the number of excitation waves is reduced, leading to the decrease of S. In Fig. 6.9 (b), also the mutual information I dependent on τ ($K = 1.0$) is plotted. Increasing the value of τ starting at $\tau = 0.0$, the time-delayed feedback control allows for pattern formation and thus for signal transmission through the net. This leads to an increase of the value of I. For values of $\tau > 0.25$, the refractory period is strongly elongated. So less wave fronts (information) can propagate through the net within a certain time and the value of I decreases. With respect to the delay time τ, the spatial cross correlation and the mutual information show a resonance-like behavior. For an intermediate value of τ, a maximal amount of information

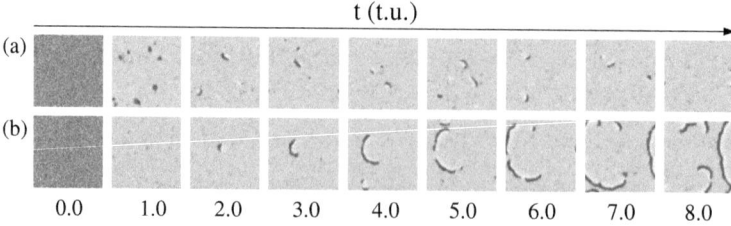

Figure 6.8: *Snapshots of the variable $u_{ij}(t)$ of a net of FHN elements [Eqs. (6.1)] for different consecutive times t. (a) Without feedback. (b) With feedback ($K = 1.0$, $\tau = 0.3\,t.u.$, $g_f = 1.0$, $\lambda_\mu = 0.0$). Gray scales as in Fig. 3.9. Random initial conditions. Further parameters: Parameter set 1, $c = 3.85$, $e = 0.0$, $N = 256$, $D_u = 50$, $\sigma_{n,e} = 0.1$, $\sigma_{v,e} = 0.0$ [79].*

6.1. SUBEXCITABLE NET OF FITZHUGH-NAGUMO ELEMENTS

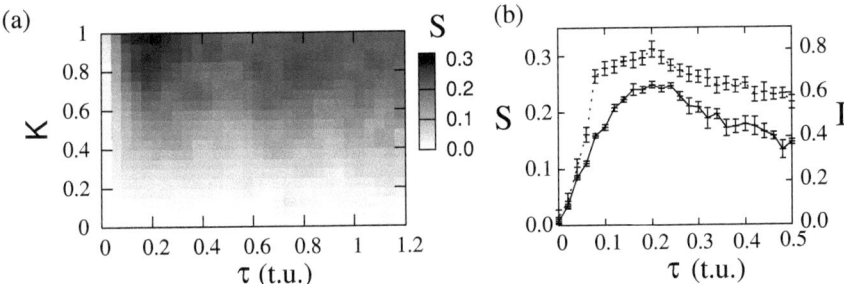

Figure 6.9: *The spatial cross correlation S [Eq. (4.15)] and the mutual information I [Eq. (4.16)] for a net of FHN elements with feedback in $v(t)$ [Eqs. (6.1)] averaged over ten realizations. (a) S dependent on K and τ. (b) ($\cdots$) S and (—) I dependent on τ for $K = 1$ [79]. Random initial conditions. Further parameters: Parameter set 1, $c = 3.85$, $e = 0.0$, $N = 256$, $D_u = 50$, $g_f = 1.0$, $\lambda_\mu = 0.0$, $\sigma_{n,e} = 0.1$, $\sigma_{v,e} = 0.0$.*

(highest number of wave fronts) can be transmitted through the net. For larger values of τ ($0.5\,t.u. < \tau \leq 1.5\,t.u.$), pattern formation is still sustained. The refractory period of the elements slowly increases further, and so the measures S and I slowly decrease, but no qualitatively new effects occur. In contrast to oscillatory nets of FHN elements, where the oscillation period ($T \approx 1.0\,t.u.$) determines an intrinsic time scale, in the homogeneous subexcitable net such a specific time scale does not exist. Hence, no special effect (e.g. resonance) for $\tau \approx 1.0\,t.u.$ is found. Generally, one can state that in subexcitable nets noise-induced patterns are sustained by time-delayed feedback for a large range of τ-values and a sufficiently large feedback strength.

In a next step, the quota g_f of the elements that get the feedback signal is varied, while the delay time is fixed at $\tau = 0.3\,t.u.$, a value, for which pattern formation is sustained for $K \gtrsim 0.4$. First the selection of the elements that get the feedback signal is done spatially uncorrelated ($\lambda_\mu = 0.0$). In Fig. 6.10, the spatial cross correlation S of the noise-induced patterns is plotted dependent on K and g_f. The coherence of the patterns increases with increasing values of K and g_f. Again one discerns the symmetric structure regarding the influence of these two feedback parameters on the pattern formation. For larger values of K, it is sufficient to control less elements via the feedback signal to sustain pattern formation and vice versa [cf. Fig. 6.6 (b)]. Again, increasing K leads to an increase of ΔB and thus less elements have to get the feedback signal to ensure that the excitations spread out (cf. subsection 6.1.1). Nevertheless, the most coherent patterns are found if all elements get the feedback signal. To manifest this result, snapshots of the variable $u_{ij}(t)$ of the net after $t = 12\,t.u.$ are composed in Fig. 6.11 dependent on K and g_f. For small values of K or g_f, the noise-induced waves die out very quickly. No waves or only very small wave fronts are visible in the snapshots of the net. If $K \gtrsim 0.4$ and $g_f \gtrsim 0.4$, pattern formation is sustained and the wave fronts can propagate through the whole net.

Next the influence of clustered control on noise-induced pattern formation is studied.

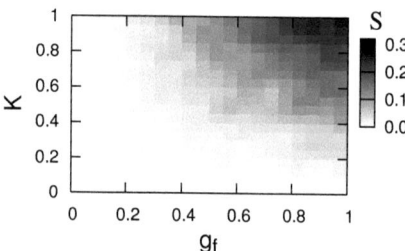

Figure 6.10: *The spatial cross correlation S [Eq. (4.15)] for a net of FHN elements with feedback in v(t) [Eqs. (6.1)] dependent on K and g_f averaged over ten realizations. Random initial conditions. Further parameters: Parameter set 1, c = 3.85, e = 0.0, N = 256, D_u = 50, τ = 0.3 t.u., λ_μ = 0.0, $\sigma_{n,e}$ = 0.1, $\sigma_{v,e}$ = 0.0 [79].*

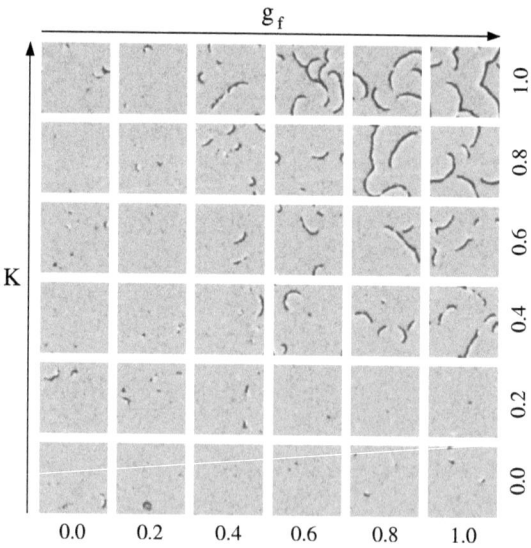

Figure 6.11: *Snapshots of the variable $u_{ij}(t)$ of a net of FHN elements with feedback in v(t) [Eqs. (6.1)] after t = 12 t.u. dependent on K and g_f. Gray scales as in Fig. 3.9. Random initial conditions. Further parameters: Parameter set 1, c = 3.85, e = 0.0, N = 256, D_u = 50, τ = 0.3 t.u., λ_μ = 0.0, $\sigma_{n,e}$ = 0.1, $\sigma_{v,e}$ = 0.0 [79].*

6.1. SUBEXCITABLE NET OF FITZHUGH-NAGUMO ELEMENTS

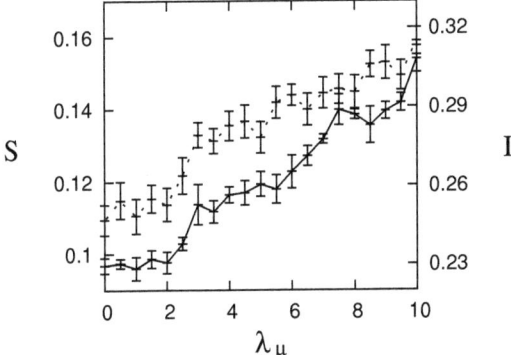

Figure 6.12: $(\cdots)$ The spatial cross correlation S [Eq. (4.15)] and (---) the mutual information I [Eq. (4.16)] for a net of FHN elements with feedback in $v(t)$ [Eqs. (6.1)] dependent on λ_μ. Average over 100 realizations. Random initial conditions. Further parameters: Parameter set 1, $c = 3.85$, $e = 0.0$, $N = 256$, $D_u = 50$, $K = 1.0$, $\tau = 0.3\,t.u.$, $g_f = 0.5$, $\sigma_{n,e} = 0.1$, $\sigma_{v,e} = 0.0$ [79].

Therefore, the feedback parameters are fixed at $K = 1.0$, $\tau = 0.3\,t.u.$, and $g_f = 0.5$. For this set of feedback parameters, pattern formation is sustained in the case of spatially uncorrelated feedback control. In Fig. 6.12, the spatial cross correlation S averaged over one hundred realizations is plotted for a varying correlation length λ_μ. For small values of the correlation length ($\lambda_\mu < 2.0$), the coherence of the noise-induced patterns is independent of λ_μ, whereas for $\lambda_\mu \gtrsim 2.0$ the measure S increases with increasing values of the correlation length. If the controlled clusters are of the size of the extension of the excitation waves, the larger clusters, which sustain pattern formation, lead to more coherent patterns in the whole net (cf. Fig. 6.7). In Fig. 6.12, also the mutual information I is plotted in dependency on λ_μ. I, a measure for the transmitted information, increases with increasing values of λ_μ similar to S. The presented results (Fig. 6.12) are the average over one hundred realizations. The results of the single simulations vary quite strongly, because the coherence of the noise-induced patterns depends on the realizations of the spatiotemporal noise and of the randomly created clusters, which are controlled via the feedback. Nevertheless, the probability that noise-induced coherent patterns emerge and that wave fronts may propagate through the whole net increases with increasing values of λ_μ for $\lambda_\mu \gtrsim 2.0$. So one can conclude that the clustered feedback control is more efficient than the spatially uncorrelated feedback control regarding the enhancement of information transmission through the net.

6.1.3 Time-Delayed Feedback Control of Variability-Induced Pattern Formation

In this subsection, the influence of time-delayed feedback on variability-induced pattern formation is studied. Variability denotes time-independent stochastic differences between the otherwise equal elements of a net. Since no noise is applied ($\sigma_{n,e} = 0.0$), the net dynamics is completely deterministic. Here only additive variability in parameter e, which is white in space [Eq. (3.19)], is considered. Whereas all other parameters have the same value as in the previous subsections, the value of parameter e now varies from element to element. The mean value of e_{ij} is $E = 0.0$. Throughout this subsection, the variability strength is fixed at $\sigma_{v,e} = 0.15$. Changing parameter e denotes a shift of the linear nullcline [see Fig. 3.2 (a)] and has thus a crucial influence on the dynamics of the single elements. In Fig. 6.13 (a), the probability distribution of the parameter e is displayed

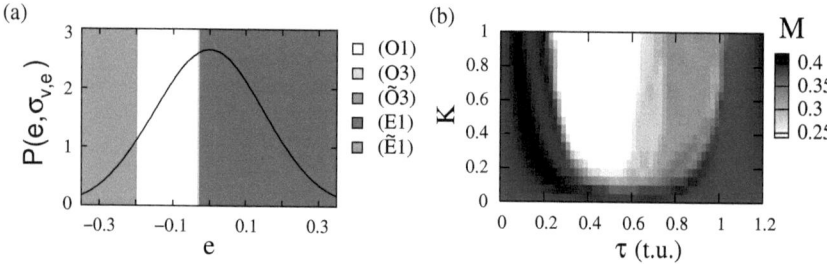

Figure 6.13: (a) (—) The Gaussian probability distribution of parameter e for $\sigma_{v,e} = 0.15$. The colored areas encode the different dynamical regimes of the single uncoupled element based on the linear stability analysis [cf. Fig 3.1 (a)]. (b) The time-average M of u(t) for a single uncoupled FHN element with feedback in v(t) [Eqs. (6.1)] dependent on the feedback parameters K and τ for $e_{ij} = -0.05$. The white region marks the amplitude death regime. Further parameters: Parameter set 1, c = 3.85, N = 1, $\sigma_{n,e} = 0.0$.

(cf. section 3.4). Based on the result of the linear stability analysis for parameter set 1 and $c = 3.85$ [cf. Fig 3.1 (a)], the colored areas of Fig. 6.13 (a) encode the different dynamical regimes of the single uncoupled elements. Thus for the given variability strength, the heterogeneous net is composed of elements in the regime $E1$ (roughly 58% of all elements), of elements in the regime $O1$ (roughly 34% of all elements), and of elements in the regime $\tilde{E}1$ (roughly 8% of all elements). Because of the large net size ($N = 256$), the quota of elements in this three different dynamical regimes is representative. The few elements in the narrow parameter regions of the regimes $O3$ and $\tilde{O}3$ do not have a crucial influence on the net dynamics and can be neglected throughout the following discussion. Without perturbations, the majority of the elements, which are in the regime $E1$, rest in their stable fixed point (lower stable fixed point). Due to the strong coupling ($D_u = 50$), also most of the elements in the regimes $O1$ and $\tilde{E}1$ are forced to remain in the lower stable fixed point. Nevertheless, with a high probability, a few small clusters of elements exist, which

6.1. SUBEXCITABLE NET OF FITZHUGH-NAGUMO ELEMENTS

oscillate. These oscillating clusters serve as excitation centers, from which excitation waves can spread out through the net. In this manner, variability can induce pattern formation [17, 19]. Because of the deterministic model equations, the patterns are periodic in time.

To understand the impact of the feedback signal on variability-induced patterns, it is essential to study first the influence of the feedback on single elements of the three different dynamical regimes. As discussed in subsection 6.1.1, for elements in the regime $E1$, the feedback causes an elongation of the duration $B(K, \tau)$ of the excitation spike, and thereby the propagation of excitation waves is improved. The impact of the feedback on elements in the regime $\tilde{E}1$ is qualitatively the same, but an excitation spike starts in the upper stable fixed point. The feedback does not change the general excitable behavior of the single elements. This is different for the oscillatory elements. As shown in the subsection 5.1.1, the feedback can stabilize the unstable focus and can cause the amplitude death of the oscillation. In Fig. 6.13 (b), the time-average M of $u(t)$ is plotted for a single oscillatory element with $e_{ij} = -0.05$ dependent on the feedback parameters K and τ. In the black region of Fig. 6.13 (b) ($M \approx 0.42$), the element performs autonomous limit cycle oscillations. The amplitude death regime [white region in Fig. 6.13 (b)] is found for $K > 0.2$ and $0.22\,t.u. < \tau < 0.63\,t.u.$ [cf. Fig. 5.2 (a)]. Here the element remains in the stabilized fixed point, which is placed close to the left stable branch of the cubic nullcline for $e_{ij} = -0.05$ [cf. Fig. 3.2 (a)]. The gray area ($0.63\,t.u. < \tau < 1.0\,t.u.$) marks a regime, where the dynamics has very long transients or shows complex oscillations with varying amplitudes.

Also within the regime $O1$, the impact of the feedback on the dynamics of the single elements depends on the value of e_{ij}. For oscillatory elements with $e_{ij} > -0.075$, the amplitude death regime is found as displayed in Fig. 6.13 (b). For $-0.075 > e_{ij} > -0.17$, the single uncoupled elements remain oscillating regardless of the feedback signal. No amplitude death regime is found. And for oscillatory elements with $e_{ij} < -0.17$, the amplitude death regime is found, but consistently, the stabilized fixed point is placed close to the right stable branch of the cubic nullcline. Thus, the feedback effectively changes the composition of the heterogeneous net.

In a next step, the influence of time-delayed feedback on the net dynamics is studied in detail. All simulations are started with random initial conditions. First, all elements get the feedback signal ($g_f = 1.0$, $\lambda_\mu = 0.0$). In Fig. 6.14, snapshots of $u_{ij}(t)$ for different consecutive times t and four different delay times τ are displayed. The feedback strength is fixed at $K = 1.0$. For all four time series, the random initial conditions and the distribution of parameter e are the same to be able to compare the development of the spatial structures. In the first row [Fig. 6.14 (a)], no feedback is present (the feedback signal vanishes for $\tau = 0.0\,t.u.$). Due to the variability in parameter e, a few small clusters of oscillating elements exist. But because of the subexcitable feature of the net, the excitations die out quickly and no waves spread out through the net. In the second row [Fig. 6.14 (b)], for $\tau = 0.16\,t.u.$ coherent patterns emerge. The small clusters of oscillating elements act as excitation centers. Due to the feedback, which elongates the duration $B(K, \tau)$ of the excitation of the elements of the regime $E1$, the excited elements can now excite their neighboring elements and the wave fronts propagate through the whole net. The fully evolved patterns [Fig. 6.14 (b) for $t = 12\,t.u.$] are periodic in time. For larger values of τ, no patterns emerge [$\tau = 0.32\,t.u.$, Fig. 6.14 (c)] and even the small oscillating clusters

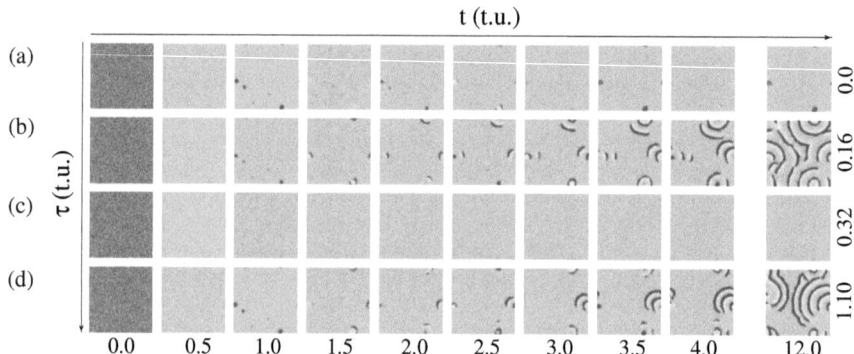

Figure 6.14: *Snapshots of the variable $u_{ij}(t)$ of a net of FHN elements with feedback in $v(t)$ [Eqs. (6.1)] for different consecutive times t. (a) $\tau = 0.0$ (without feedback). (b) $\tau = 0.16\,t.u.$ (c) $\tau = 0.32\,t.u.$ (d) $\tau = 1.1\,t.u.$ Gray scales as in Fig. 3.9. The random initial conditions and the distribution of parameter e are identical for (a)-(d). Further parameters: Parameter set 1, $c = 3.85$, $E = 0.0$, $N = 256$, $D_u = 50$, $K = 1.0$, $g_f = 1.0$, $\lambda_\mu = 0.0$, $\sigma_{n,e} = 0.0$, $\sigma_{v,e} = 0.15$.*

have vanished. This is due to the fact that a part of the oscillatory elements is in the amplitude death regime [Fig. 6.13 (b)]. And the remaining oscillatory elements are not able to constitute oscillating clusters. For larger values of τ, again pattern formation is sustained by the feedback [$\tau = 1.1\,t.u.$, Fig. 6.14 (d)]. The oscillatory elements are not affected by the feedback signal, since τ is close to the oscillation period. Thus small oscillating clusters exist, which serve as excitation centers of the wave fronts. The duration $B(K, \tau)$ of the excitation of the elements of the regime $E1$ is still prolonged so that the propagation of the wave fronts is sustained.

To measure the influence of the feedback signal on variability-induced pattern formation in the subexcitable net, the spatial cross correlation S [Eq. (4.15)] is used. In Fig. 6.15 (a), S is plotted dependent on the feedback parameters K and τ for $g_f = 1.0$ averaged over ten realizations. For small values of τ ($\tau \leq 0.05\,t.u.$), the variability-induced wave fronts die out very quickly [cf. Fig. 6.14 (a)], and thus the value of S is close to zero. In the range of $0.05\,t.u. < \tau < 0.25\,t.u.$, pattern formation is sustained for large enough values of K [cf. Fig. 6.14 (b)]. The coherence of the patterns increases with increasing values of K and τ. In this range of τ-values, the dynamical behavior is quite similar to the case of noise-induced patterns (see subsection 6.1.2). In difference to the noise-induced patterns, where wave fronts can be excited anywhere in the net, the variability-induced patterns have steady excitation centers. Nevertheless, the effect that the feedback signal sustains the propagation of the wave fronts is the same for both cases. For larger values of τ ($0.25\,t.u. < \tau < 0.9\,t.u.$), a great difference between noise- and variability-induced patterns arises. Whereas for noise-induced patterns, coherent structures are found for $K > 0.4$ [cf. Fig. 6.9 (a)], in the case of variability, the probability that patterns emerge is

6.2. SUBEXCITABLE NET OF HODGKIN-HUXLEY ELEMENTS

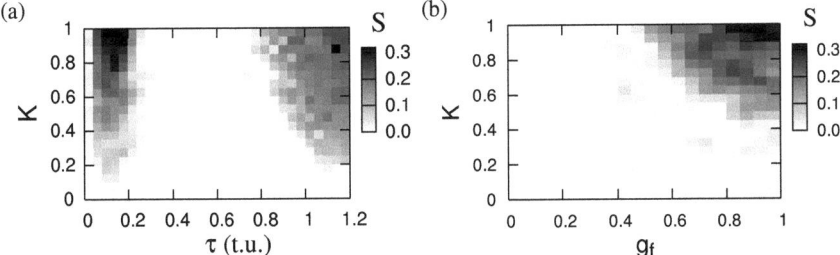

Figure 6.15: *The spatial cross correlation S [Eq. (4.15)] for a net of FHN elements with feedback in $v(t)$ [Eqs. (6.1)] averaged over ten realizations. (a) Dependent on K and τ for $g_f = 1.0$. (b) Dependent on K and g_f for $\tau = 0.16\,t.u.$. Random initial conditions. Further parameters: Parameter set 1, $c = 3.85$, $E = 0.0$, $N = 256$, $D_u = 50$, $\lambda_\mu = 0.0$, $\sigma_{n,e} = 0.0$, $\sigma_{v,e} = 0.15$.*

almost zero. Thus S is close to zero as visible in Fig. 6.15 (a). In this range of τ-values, a reasonable number of oscillatory elements are in the amplitude death regime. Thus, the probability that large enough oscillating clusters exist to act as excitation center, is vanishing. For intermediate values of τ, it is crucial whether the excitation waves are induced by noise or by variability. For large values of τ ($\tau \gtrsim 0.9\,t.u.$) and $K \gtrsim 0.3$, again patterns emerge, yielding larger values of S. The explanation is the same as given above for Fig. 6.14 (d).

Next the quota g_f of the elements that get the feedback signal is varied. Therefore, the delay time is fixed at $\tau = 0.16\,t.u.$, a value, for which pattern formation is sustained for $K \gtrsim 0.4$. The selection of the elements that get the feedback signal is done spatially uncorrelated ($\lambda_\mu = 0.0$). In Fig. 6.15 (b), the spatial cross correlation S of the variability-induced patterns is plotted dependent on K and g_f. The coherence of the patterns increases with increasing values of K and g_f. For larger values of K, it is sufficient to control less elements via the feedback signal to sustain pattern formation and vice versa. Nevertheless, the most coherent patterns are found if all elements get the feedback signal. Since the oscillatory elements are not disturbed by the feedback signal for the given value of τ, the result is pretty similar to the case of noise-induced patterns [cf. Fig. 6.10]. The explanation is given there.

6.2 Subexcitable Net of Hodgkin-Huxley Elements

In this section, the influence of time-delayed feedback on the propagation of wave fronts for nets of HH elements is investigated. Similar to a net of FHN elements, a net of excitable HH elements (regime $E1$) can show subexcitable or excitable behavior. For the HH models only the propagation of wave fronts induced by special initial conditions is studied. The net size is $N = 200$. To discern subexcitable and excitable net dynamics, throughout this section the life time T_L of a wave front serves as order parameter. The life time T_L of a

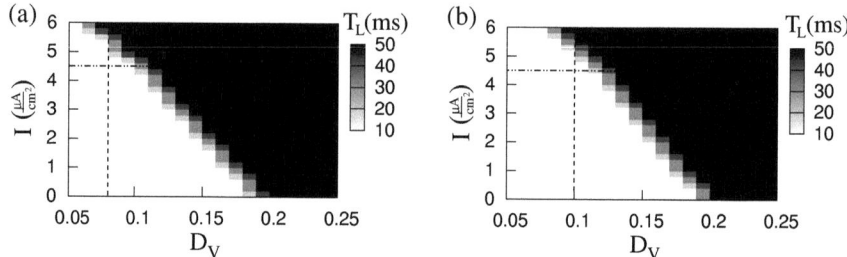

Figure 6.16: *The life time T_L of a wave front induced by special initial conditions for a net of HH elements without feedback dependent on I and D_V. (a) For the reduced HH model [Eqs. (3.13)], ($----$) $D_V = 0.08$, ($-\cdot\cdot-$) $I = 4.5\frac{\mu A}{cm^2}$. (b) For the full HH model [Eqs. (3.12)], ($----$) $D_V = 0.1$, ($-\cdot\cdot-$) $I = 4.5\frac{\mu A}{cm^2}$. The black colored area ($T_L \geq 50\,ms$) marks the excitable regime, else ($T_L < 50\,ms$) the subexcitable regime. Further parameters: Parameters given by Eq. (3.7), $N = 200$, $K = 0.0$.*

wave front induced by special initial conditions is defined as the largest time, for which $V_{ij}(t) > -30\,mV$ is found at least for one of the $N \times N$ elements.

First, the net dynamics is studied without feedback. Whether a wave front spreads out or shrinks, depends on the bifurcation parameter I and on the coupling strength D_V. In Fig. 6.16 (a), the life time T_L is plotted dependent on I and D_V for the reduced HH model [Eqs. (3.13)]. The total integration time is $T = 50\,ms$. If the life time achieves $T_L = 50\,ms$ [black area in Fig. 6.16 (a)], the wave front propagates through the whole net (excitable behavior). If the wave front dies out ($T_L < 50\,ms$), the net is subexcitable. In the subexcitable regime, for almost all parameter values the wave fronts die out very quickly ($T_L < 10\,ms$). Since the transition from $T_L < 10\,ms$ to $T_L \geq 50\,ms$ is quite sharp, the life time is an appropriate order parameter to qualify the net dynamics and a total integration time of $T = 50\,ms$ is sufficient. The subexcitable regime is only found for very small coupling strengths compared to the phenomenon of amplitude death (cf. subsection 5.2.2).

For a net of HH elements obeying the full model equations [Eqs. (3.12)], the border between the subexcitable and the excitable regime is slightly shifted to larger values of D_V [Fig. 6.16 (b)]. In both panels, the parameter values of I and D_V, which are used for all following simulations, are marked by the dashed-dotted and the dashed line, respectively. For the reduced model, the parameters are $I = 4.5\frac{\mu A}{cm^2}$ and $D_V = 0.08$. All further simulations of the full model equations are done for $I = 4.5\frac{\mu A}{cm^2}$ and $D_V = 0.1$.

Now feedback is considered. Throughout this section, only local feedback applied to the gating variable $n(t)$ is investigated. Feedback in the potential variable $V(t)$ reveals no qualitatively new results. First, the impact of the feedback signal on a single uncoupled element is studied. In Figs. 6.17 (a) and 6.17 (b), the measure ΔB [Eq. (4.19)] is plotted in dependency on the feedback parameters K and τ for the reduced and the full HH model, respectively. For both models, the duration $B(K,\tau)$ of the excitation increases with increasing values of K and τ. This is similar to the behavior found for the FHN

6.2. SUBEXCITABLE NET OF HODGKIN-HUXLEY ELEMENTS

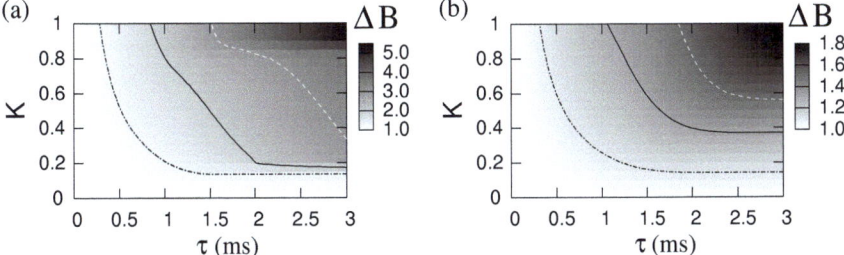

Figure 6.17: ΔB [Eq. (4.19)] for a single uncoupled HH element with feedback in the gating variable $n(t)$ dependent on K and τ. (a) For the reduced HH model [Eqs. (3.13)], $(-\cdot-)$ $\Delta B = 1.3$, $(—)$ $\Delta B = 2.0$, $(---)$ $\Delta B = 3.0$. (b) For the full HH model [Eqs. (3.12)], $(-\cdot-)$ $\Delta B = 1.1$, $(—)$ $\Delta B = 1.3$, $(---)$ $\Delta B = 1.5$. Further parameters: Parameters given by Eq. (3.7), $I = 4.5 \frac{\mu A}{cm^2}$, $N = 1$, $g_f = 1.0$.

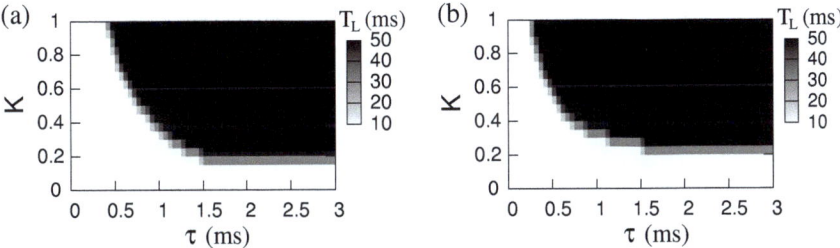

Figure 6.18: The life time T_L of a wave front induced by special initial conditions for a net of HH elements with feedback in the gating variable $n(t)$ dependent on K and τ. (a) For the reduced model [Eqs. (3.13)], $D_V = 0.08$. (b) For the full model [Eqs. (3.12)], $D_V = 0.1$. The black area $(T_L \geq 50\,ms)$ marks the excitable regime, else $(T_L < 50\,ms)$ the subexcitable regime. Further parameters: Parameters given by Eq. (3.7), $I = 4.5 \frac{\mu A}{cm^2}$, $N = 200$, $g_f = 1.0$, $\lambda_\mu = 0.0$.

model [cf. Fig. 6.4 (a)].

Regarding the net dynamics, the elongation of the duration of the excitation may have a crucial influence. The life time T_L of a wave front induced by special initial conditions is plotted dependent on K and τ in Fig. 6.18. Again one gets similar results for both, the reduced [Fig. 6.18 (a)] and the full HH model [Fig. 6.18 (b)]. For small values of K and τ, the wave front dies out. The net is subexcitable. If the values of K and τ are large enough so that the duration $B(K,\tau)$ of the excitation exceeds a certain value, the wave front propagates through the whole net $(T_L \geq 50\,ms)$. The feedback sustains the propagation of wave fronts and thus allows for signal transmission through subexcitable nets of HH elements. The explanation is the same as discussed above for the FHN model

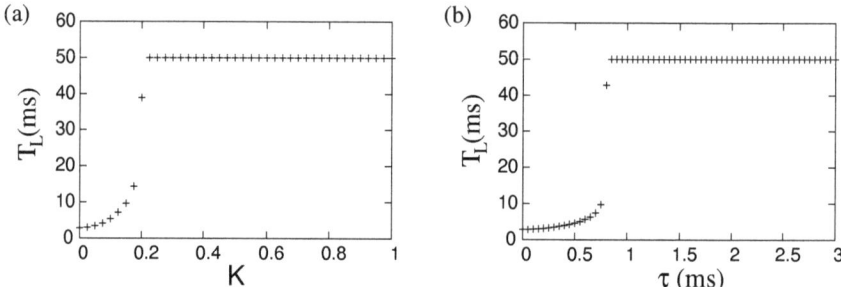

Figure 6.19: *The life time T_L of a wave front induced by special initial conditions for a net of reduced HH elements with feedback in the gating variable $n(t)$ [Eqs. (3.13)]. (a) Dependent on K for $\tau = 2.0\,ms$. (b) Dependent on τ for $K = 0.5$. $T_L \geq 50\,ms$ denotes excitable behavior, else $(T_L < 50\,ms)$ subexcitable behavior. Further parameters: Parameters given by Eq. (3.7), $I = 4.5\frac{\mu A}{cm^2}$, $N = 200$, $D_V = 0.08$, $g_f = 1.0$, $\lambda_\mu = 0.0$.*

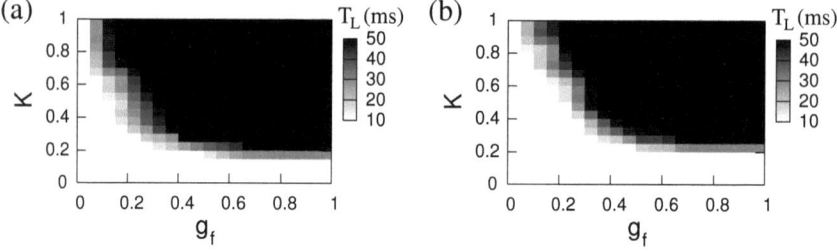

Figure 6.20: *The life time T_L of a wave front induced by special initial conditions for a net of HH elements with feedback in the gating variable $n(t)$ dependent on K and g_f. (a) For the reduced model [Eqs. (3.13)], $D_V = 0.08$. (b) For the full model [Eqs. (3.12)], $D_V = 0.1$. The black area $(T_L \geq 50\,ms)$ marks the excitable regime, else $(T_L < 50\,ms)$ the subexcitable regime. Further parameters: Parameters given by Eq. (3.7), $I = 4.5\frac{\mu A}{cm^2}$, $N = 200$, $\tau = 2.0\,ms$, $\lambda_\mu = 0.0$.*

[cf. subsection 6.1.1]. The duration of the excitation of the excited elements at the edge of the wave front determines whether they can excite their neighboring elements. If the duration of the excitation is large enough, the wave front grows and spreads out. Thus even for the quite complex HH models, time-delayed feedback can cause a transition from subexcitable to excitable net dynamics, which is quite sharp similar to the transition for varying I and D_V (cf. Fig. 6.16). In Fig. 6.19, sections of the Fig. 6.18 (a) (reduced HH model) are shown. The panels (a) and (b) of Fig. 6.19 demonstrate that the transition from subexcitable to excitable net dynamics is quite sharp regarding an increase of both, the feedback strength K and the delay time τ.

6.2. SUBEXCITABLE NET OF HODGKIN-HUXLEY ELEMENTS

Finally, the influence of the quota g_f of elements that get the feedback signal on the propagation of a wave front is investigated. The elements that get the feedback signal are spatially uncorrelated ($\lambda_\mu = 0.0$). For both models, the delay time τ is fixed at $\tau = 2.0\,ms$. The impact of the feedback parameters K and g_f on the propagation of wave fronts is qualitatively the same for the reduced [Fig. 6.20 (a)] and the full HH model [Fig. 6.20 (b)]. For larger values of K, it is sufficient to control a smaller quota g_f of all elements to reach the excitable regime. An increasing K results in an increasing ΔB [Figs. 6.17 (a) and 6.17 (b), respectively]. Consequently, for larger values of K less elements at the edge of a wave front have to be controlled via the feedback signal to ensure the excitation of their neighboring elements and the propagation of an excitation wave (cf. subsection 6.1.1).

Summarizing, in this chapter it is shown that time-delayed feedback sustains pattern formation in subexcitable nets of FHN and HH elements. Regarding wave fronts induced by special initial conditions or noise-induced wave fronts, excitability is induced for a large range of feedback parameters. For variability-induced wave fronts however additionally regions of the delay time τ exist, where any excitations are suppressed.

Chapter 7

Influence of Variability and Noise on the Net Dynamics of Bistable FitzHugh-Nagumo Elements

It is well-known that both, noise and variability, can play a constructive role in nonlinear systems. Examples are: *Noise- and variability-induced phase transitions* [9, 10, 38, 70]; *stochastic resonance* [14]; *coherence resonance* [31]; *spatiotemporal stochastic resonance* [32, 33]; *array-enhanced coherence resonance* [80]. Stochastic resonance was found in many different physical, chemical and biological systems [7, 8, 14, 81]. For instance, the balance control of humans is enhanced using the stochastic resonance effect [8]. The constructive role of noise is up to now a topic of great interest. Doubly stochastic effects are investigated [82, 83]. It is shown that the output signal of a bistable neural element is most coherent at an intermediate strength of additive and multiplicative noise [83]. In spatially extended systems, often noise can be replaced by variability yielding the same effects on the dynamical behavior [17, 23, 38]. Recently, it was shown that variability can induce a resonant collective behavior in a chain of coupled bistable or excitable elements, which are driven by an external signal (*diversity-induced resonance*, the counterpart of stochastic resonance) [21, 22, 23].

Many physical, chemical or biological systems show bistable behavior. Bistable systems play, for example, an important role for memory devices. Other examples are so called flip-flop circuits (Eccles-Jordan trigger circuit [84]) in the field of electrical engineering or the Schlögl reaction [85], a bistable chemical reaction. In this chapter, the dynamics of bistable FHN elements is studied. For all simulations the parameter set 2 [Eq. (3.4)] is used. First the influence of noise and variability is investigated. Then the response of a net of FHN elements to a weak periodic signal is studied. It is shown that the response of the net at the external driving frequency reveals a resonance-like dependency on the noise and variability strengths (stochastic and variability-induced resonance). In the last section, an outlook is given where the influence of time-delayed feedback on the stochastic resonance effect is discussed.

7.1 Dynamics of a Single Element

Throughout this chapter, a net of FHN elements with variability and noise in the parameters c and e [Eqs. (3.16)] is considered. Due to the variability, the parameter values of c and e differ from element to element. To understand the net dynamics, first the dynamics of a single uncoupled element (ij-element) is investigated dependent on its parameter values of c_{ij} and e_{ij}. First the influence of the parameter value c_{ij} is discussed, where e_{ij} is fixed at $e_{ij} = -0.2$. For the parameter value $c_{ij} = 7.3$, the stability analyses shows that a single uncoupled element is in the bistable regime [Fig. 3.1 (b), regime B]. The parameter c_{ij} determines the slope of the linear nullcline and thereby the thresholds for a transition between the two stable fixed points, which has a crucial influence on the dynamics of the single element. In Fig. 7.1 (a), the nullclines are plotted for different values of parameter c_{ij}. Decreasing the parameter c_{ij} from 7.3 to 6.2 the single element remains in the bistable regime [Fig. 3.1 (b)]. But the threshold for a transition from the upper to the lower stable fixed point becomes smaller, while the threshold for the inverse transition persists unchanged.

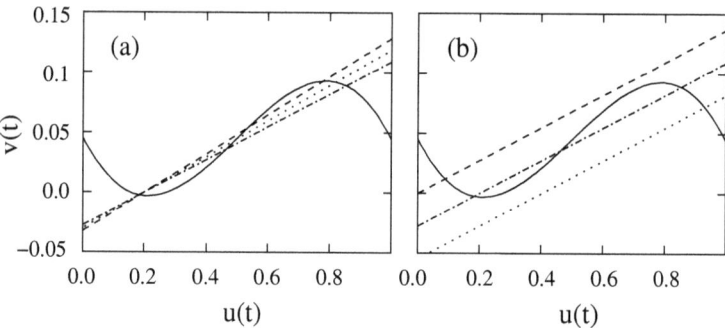

Figure 7.1: Phase space plot with nullclines of a single uncoupled FHN element [Eqs. (3.11)]. (—) cubic nullcline. (a) Linear nullclines for $e_{ij} = -0.2$ and three different values of c_{ij}. (– · –) $c_{ij} = 7.3$, (· · ·) $c_{ij} = 6.7$, (– – –) $c_{ij} = 6.2$. (b) Linear nullclines for $c_{ij} = 7.3$ and three different values of e_{ij}. (– – –) $e_{ij} = 0.0$, (– · –) $e_{ij} = -0.2$, (· · ·) $e_{ij} = -0.4$. Further parameters: Parameter set 2 [23].

This behavior can be demonstrated by applying additive noise. In Fig. 7.2, time series of $u_{ij}(t)$ of the ij-element are shown for three different values of parameter c_{ij}, where weak additive noise ($\sigma_{n,e} = 0.02$) induces jumps between the two stable states. For $c_{ij} = 7.3$, the system spends roughly all the time in the upper stable fixed point [Fig. 7.2 (a)]. The threshold for a transition from the upper stable fixed point to the lower stable fixed point is larger than the threshold for the inverse transition. This case is called the asymmetric bistable regime troughout this chapter. For $c_{ij} = 6.7$, the system spends roughly the same time in both stable states [Fig. 7.2 (b)]. So, the thresholds for transitions between the two stable fixed points are approximately of the same size (symmetric bistable regime). For

7.1. DYNAMICS OF A SINGLE ELEMENT

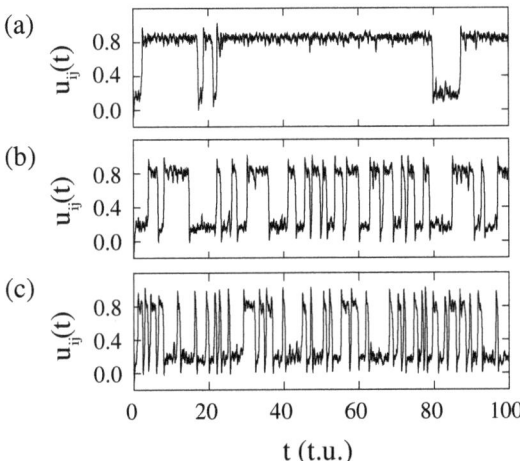

Figure 7.2: *Time series of $u_{ij}(t)$ of a single uncoupled FHN element [Eqs. (3.11)] for different parameters c_{ij} driven by weak additive noise ($\sigma_{n,e} = 0.02$). (a) $c_{ij} = 7.3$, (b) $c_{ij} = 6.7$, (c) $c_{ij} = 6.2$. Further parameters: Parameter set 2, $e_{ij} = -0.2$ [23].*

$c_{ij} = 6.2$, the threshold for a transition from the upper stable fixed point to the lower stable fixed point is smaller than the threshold for the inverse transition, the system prefers to stay in the lower state [Fig. 7.2 (c)].

With variability, the net is a mixture of FHN elements in different dynamical regimes. Multiplicative variability ($\sigma_{v,c} > 0.0$) is applied with parameter values c_{ij}, which are Gaussian distributed and white in space [Eq. (3.20)] with fixed mean $C = 7.3$. In Fig. 7.3 (a), the distribution of parameter c is plotted for two different values of the variability strength $\sigma_{v,c}$ [$\sigma_{v,c} = 1.0, 2.0$], where the colored areas encode the different dynamical regimes of the single uncoupled elements based on the linear stability analysis [cf. Fig 3.1 (b), $e = -0.2$, $\sigma_{v,e} = 0.0$]. For $c_{ij} < 0$, the slope of the linear nullcline is negative and the dynamics of the element changes completely. Consequently, these parameter values have to be excluded by setting the probability distribution $P(c, \sigma_{v,c})$ equal to zero for $c < 0$. To ensure that the mean value remains $C = 7.3$, the cut-off is done symmetrically. That means that the probability distribution $P(c, \sigma_{v,c})$ is also set equal to zero for $c > 2C$. For $\sigma_{v,c} = 4.0$, the largest variability strength used in this thesis, less than 6.5% of the Gaussian distributed c_{ij} are excluded.

Now the influence of the parameter value e_{ij} on the dynamics of a single uncoupled element is discussed, where c_{ij} is fixed at $c_{ij} = 7.3$. The parameter e_{ij} determines the position of the linear nullcline regarding the v-axis [Fig. 7.1 (b)] and thereby the dynamical regime ($E1$, B or $\tilde{E}1$) of the single element. Within the bistable regime, the thresholds for a transition between the two stable fixed points depend crucially on the value of e_{ij}. In Fig. 7.3 (b), the distribution of parameter e is plotted for two different values of the

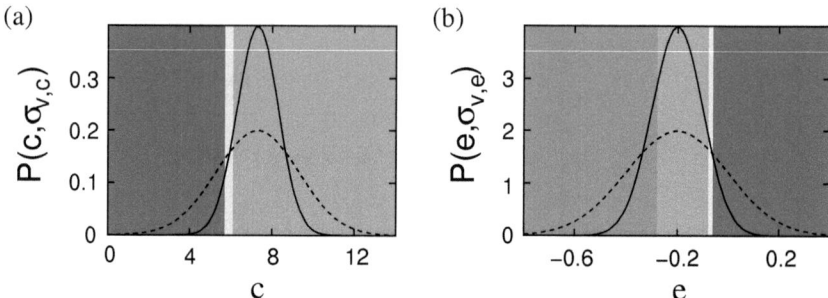

Figure 7.3: (a) The Gaussian probability distribution $P(c, \sigma_{v,c})$ of parameter c for $\sigma_{v,c} = 1.0$ (—) and $\sigma_{v,c} = 2.0$ (- - -). $\sigma_{v,e} = 0.0$. (b) The Gaussian probability distribution $P(e, \sigma_{v,e})$ of parameter e for $\sigma_{v,e} = 0.1$ (—) and $\sigma_{v,e} = 0.2$ (- - -). $\sigma_{v,c} = 0.0$. The colored areas encode the different dynamical regimes of the single uncoupled element based on the linear stability analysis [cf. Fig 3.1 (b)]. Further parameters: Parameter set 2, $C = 7.3$, $E = -0.2$.

variability strength $\sigma_{v,e}$ [$\sigma_{v,e} = 0.1, 0.2$], where the colored areas again encode the different dynamical regimes of the single uncoupled elements based on the linear stability analysis [cf. Fig 3.1 (b), $c = 7.3$, $\sigma_{v,c} = 0.0$]. For $e_{ij} > -0.07$ and $c_{ij} = 7.3$ the single uncoupled element is in the regime $E1$, and for $e_{ij} < -0.27$ and $c_{ij} = 7.3$ in the regime $\tilde{E}1$, respectively [cf. Fig. 7.1 (b)].

Regardless of the heterogeneity of a net with variability, due to the strong coupling ($D_u = 20$), the net shows always bistable dynamics at least for those values of additive and multiplicative variability, which are applied in the simulations presented in this chapter. For all further simulations, parameter E is fixed at $E = -0.2$.

7.2 Noise- and Variability-Induced Symmetry

In this section, the influence of multiplicative noise and multiplicative variability on the dynamics of a net of bistable FHN elements is studied. The net size is $N = 256$ and the coupling strength is $D_u = 20$ [cf. Fig. 5.10 (a)]. Both values are sufficiently large to observe the systematic influence of the multiplicative stochastic forces. It has been shown that multiplicative variability can systematically change the net dynamics, similar to multiplicative noise [19, 38]. The net dynamics can be predicted by introducing the effective parameters c_{SNE} [Eq. (4.4)] and c_{eff} [Eq. (4.7)] for multiplicative noise and multiplicative variability, respectively. To quantify the net dynamics, the time-averaged mean field M [Eq. (4.12)] is used. Throughout this section, no additive variability is applied ($\sigma_{v,e} = 0.0$), whereas additive noise ($\sigma_{n,e} = 0.1$) is present to induce transitions between the two stable states.

First, the net dynamics of a homogeneous net ($\sigma_{v,c} = 0.0$) without multiplicative noise ($\sigma_{n,c} = 0.0$) is studied dependent on parameter c. In Fig. 7.4 (a), the order parameter

7.2. NOISE- AND VARIABILITY-INDUCED SYMMETRY

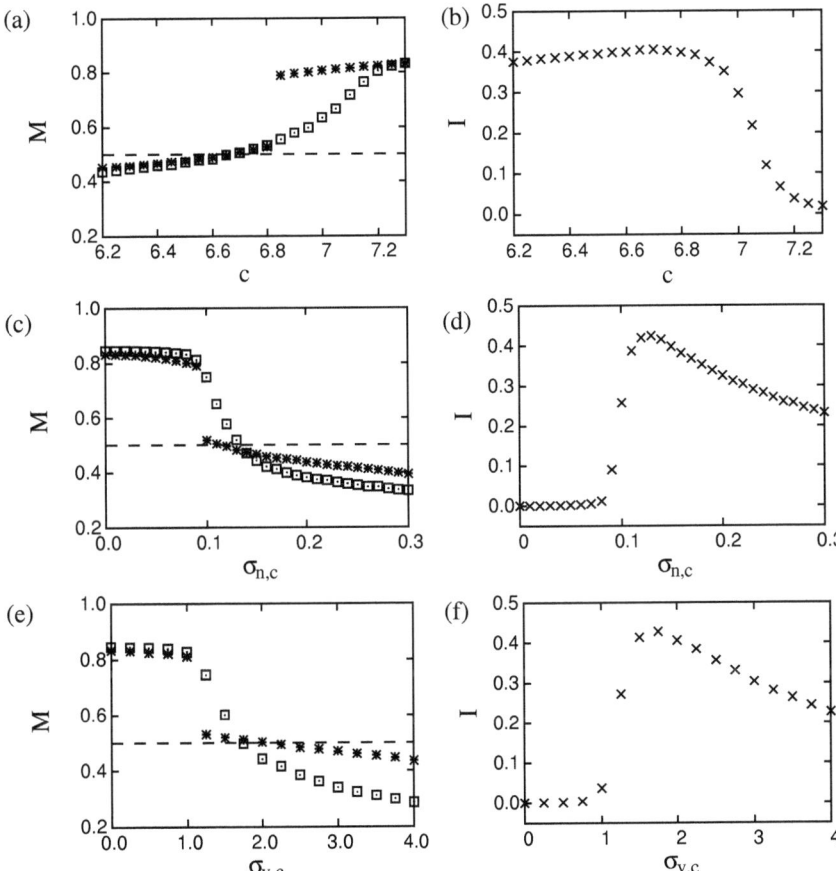

Figure 7.4: (a),(c),(e) The time-averaged mean field M [Eq. (4.12)] for a net of FHN elements [Eqs. (3.16)] for global (stars) and diffusive coupling (squares). $(---)$ $M = 0.5$. (b),(d),(f) The mutual information I [Eq. (4.16)] of a diffusively coupled net of FHN elements. (a),(b) Dependent on parameter c ($\sigma_{n,c} = 0.0$, $\sigma_{v,c} = 0.0$). (c),(d) Dependent on $\sigma_{n,c}$ ($c = 7.3$, $\sigma_{v,c} = 0.0$). (e),(f) Dependent on $\sigma_{v,c}$ ($C = 7.3$, $\sigma_{n,c} = 0.0$). Further parameters: Parameter set 2, $e = -0.2$, $N = 256$, $D_u = 20$, $\sigma_{v,e} = 0.0$, $\sigma_{n,e} = 0.1$.

M is plotted dependent on parameter c for both, global coupling and diffusive coupling. The time series with a total integration time of $T = 400\,t.u.$ are quite long to obtain a representative value of M. If all elements remain in the lower stable fixed point for all times, $M \approx 0.2$, the u-coordinate of the lower fixed point. If all elements remain in the upper stable fixed point for all times, $M \approx 0.8$, the u-coordinate of the upper fixed point. For $c = 6.2$, due to the additive noise the elements jump between the two stable states, but in average they remain longer in the lower stable state ($M \approx 0.42 < 0.5$). With an increasing value of c, M increases. For $c = 6.7$, the symmetric bistable regime is realized. All elements of the net remain the same time in both stable fixed points [$M = 0.5$, dashed line in Fig. 7.4 (a)]. Finally, for $c = 7.3$, all elements remain in the upper stable fixed point. The threshold for a transition from the upper stable fixed point to the lower stable fixed point is much larger than the threshold for the inverse transition (asymmetric bistable regime). For the given noise strength, almost no transitions from the upper to the lower stable state occur. The behavior of M is qualitatively the same for globally and diffusively coupled nets. But whereas in globally coupled nets all elements jump synchronously between the two stable states, in diffusively coupled nets patterns emerge. That is the reason why the transition to large values of M for $c \geq 6.9$ occurs smoother for the diffusive coupling.

To analyse the pattern formation in diffusively coupled nets, the mutual information I [Eq. (4.16)] is calculated. The result is plotted in Fig. 7.4 (b). For intermediate values of c ($c \approx 6.7$, symmetric bistable regime), one finds the most coherent patterns (maximum of I). To illustrate the pattern formation, which is induced by the additive noise, snapshots of the diffusively coupled net after $t = 100\,t.u.$ for different parameter values of c are composed in Fig. 7.5 (a). For large values of c ($c \geq 6.8$), the area of attraction of the upper stable state dominates the net dynamics. If the noise drives some elements into the lower stable state, these elements pull their neighboring elements into the lower stable state. But due to the asymmetric thresholds, the elements quickly return to the upper stable fixed point. So, the jump to the lower stable fixed point and back propagates like an excitation wave through the net. The same dynamical behavior just exchanging the meaning of the two stable fixed points is found for small values of c ($c \leq 6.6$). Here the jump from the lower to the upper stable fixed point and back spreads out like an excitation wave. The patterns can not be distinguished from noise-induced wave fronts in an excitable net, which is realized for $c \leq 6.1$. For $c \approx 6.7$ (symmetric bistable regime), the pattern consists of wave fronts, where the black and light gray ones have the same thickness. Here the mutual information is maximal [cf. Fig. 7.4 (b)], the patterns are most coherent.

Next the influence of multiplicative noise without variability ($\sigma_{v,c} = 0.0$) is studied. The SNE predicts a decrease of the value of the effective parameter c_{SNE} with an increasing noise strength [Eq. (4.4)]. Starting in the asymmetric bistable regime [$c = 7.3$, cf. Fig. 7.2 (a)], one expects a transition towards the symmetric bistable regime and further towards the excitable behavior (regime $E1$). In Fig. 7.4 (c), the time-averaged mean field M is plotted dependent on the noise strength $\sigma_{n,c}$ again for both types of coupling. For small values of $\sigma_{n,c}$, the net is in the asymmetric bistable regime and the additive noise rarely induce jumps from the upper to the lower stable state ($M \approx 0.8$). Increasing $\sigma_{n,c}$, the elements are jumping more frequently between the two stable states and the value of M decreases, the elements remain longer and longer in the lower stable state.

7.2. NOISE- AND VARIABILITY-INDUCED SYMMETRY

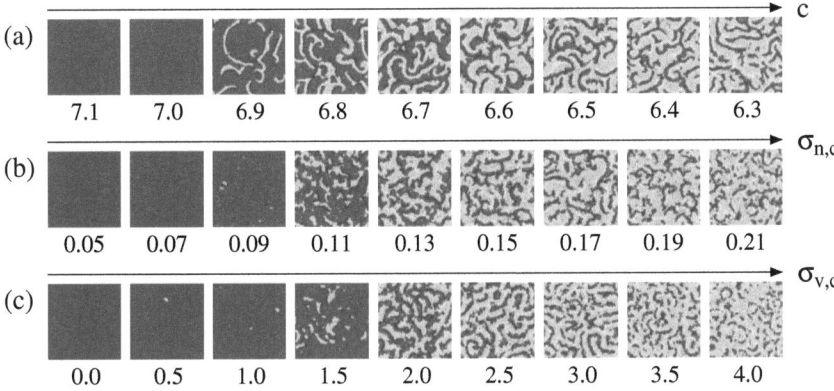

Figure 7.5: *Snapshots of the variable $u_{ij}(t)$ of a diffusively coupled net of FHN elements [Eqs. (3.16)] after $t = 100\,t.u.$ (a) For different values of c ($\sigma_{n,c} = 0.0$, $\sigma_{v,c} = 0.0$). (b) For different values of $\sigma_{n,c}$ ($c = 7.3$, $\sigma_{v,c} = 0.0$). (c) For different values of $\sigma_{v,c}$ ($C = 7.3$, $\sigma_{n,c} = 0.0$). Further parameters: Parameter set 2, $e = -0.2$, $N = 256$, $D_u = 20$, $\sigma_{v,e} = 0.0$, $\sigma_{n,e} = 0.1$.*

For intermediate values of $\sigma_{n,c}$, the elements remain the same time in both stable states ($M = 0.5$), the symmetric bistable regime is induced by the multiplicative noise with $\sigma_{n,c} \approx 0.13$. The effect of noise-induced symmetry occurs for both types of coupling. For global coupling, the symmetric bistable regime is reached for a slightly smaller value of $\sigma_{n,c}$ as for the diffusive coupling. Following the SNE, a noise strength of $\sigma_{n,c} = 0.13$ leads to an effective parameter value of $c_{SNE} \approx 6.85$, which is quite close to $c = 6.7$, the value for which the symmetric bistable behavior is found in the homogeneous deterministic case. Again, the most coherent patterns are found for the symmetric bistable regime [$\sigma_{n,c} \approx 0.13$, Fig. 7.4 (d)]. Following the snapshots of the diffusively coupled net with increasing noise strength [Fig. 7.5 (b)], one discerns clearly the transition towards the symmetric bistable regime and further to the regime, where the area of attraction of the lower stable fixed point dominates the pattern formation. In comparison to Fig. 7.5 (a), it is obvious that an increase of the multiplicative noise strength causes qualitatively a decrease of parameter c, as predicted by the SNE.

Now the influence of multiplicative variability on the net dynamics is investigated ($C = 7.3$, $\sigma_{n,c} = 0.0$). Calculating the mean gradient angle (see section 4.2), one obtains an effective parameter c_{eff} [Eq. (4.7)] that describes the systematic influence of the multiplicative variability. In Fig. 7.6, the effective parameter c_{eff} is plotted in dependency on the variability strength $\sigma_{v,c}$. The effective parameter decreases with an increasing variability strength. Thus, one expects a transition towards the symmetric bistable regime and further towards the excitable behavior (regime $E1$), similar as for multiplicative noise. In Fig. 7.4 (e), M is plotted dependent on the variability strength $\sigma_{v,c}$ again for both types

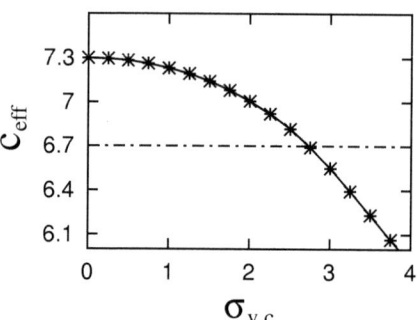

Figure 7.6: *Systematic influence of the multiplicative variability [Eq. (4.7)]: (—) The effective parameter c_{eff} dependent on $\sigma_{v,c}$. (stars) The specific values of $\sigma_{v,c}$ used for the simulations. $(-\cdot-)$ $c = 6.7$, corresponds to the symmetric bistable regime [23].*

of coupling. Here, the symmetric bistable regime is found for $\sigma_{v,c} \approx 2.0$ for the global coupling and for a slightly smaller value ($\sigma_{v,c} \approx 1.75$) for the diffusive coupling. As Fig. 7.6 shows, an increase of the variability strength $\sigma_{v,c}$ leads to a steeper slope averaged over the linear nullcline of all elements (smaller value of c_{eff}), and thereby the mean threshold (threshold averaged over all elements) for a transition from the upper to the lower stable state becomes smaller. The decrease of the effective parameter c_{eff} [$c_{eff}(\sigma_{v,c} = 2.0) \approx 7.0$] shows that the system is shifted towards the symmetric bistable regime ($c = 6.7$). The quantitative agreement is even better for nets with stronger coupling. Hence, multiplicative variability has a systematic influence on the net dynamics and may completely change the dynamical behavior of a system as multiplicative noise can do. Regarding the diffusively coupled net, the mutual information shows a resonance-like dependency on the variability strength [Fig. 7.4 (f)]. Again, the most coherent patterns are found for intermediate values of $\sigma_{v,c}$, where the symmetric bistable regime is induced. Comparing the snapshots composed in Fig. 7.5 (c) with these of Fig. 7.5 (b), one clearly discerns that multiplicative noise can be replaced by multiplicative variability to induce a systematic change of the net dynamics. In the symmetric bistable regime, the pattern consists of wave fronts, where both stable states are equally participated [Fig. 7.5 (c) for $\sigma_{v,c} = 2.0$]. The black and light gray colored wave fronts have again the same thickness [cf. Fig. 7.5 (a) and Fig. 7.5 (b)].

The variability strength to induce the symmetric bistable regime is roughly one order of magnitude larger than the corresponding noise the strength. That the variability strength has to be approximately ten times larger than the noise strength to yield comparable systematic effects on the dynamics of spatially extended systems, is confirmed by other investigations [19, 38, 39]. Unfortunately, this scaling between the noise and the variability strengths could not be explained yet.

7.3 Variability-Induced Resonance

In this section, the response of a net of bistable FHN elements to a weak external signal in presence of the additive stochastic forces is investigated. Considering a periodic signal acting on the slow variable $v(t)$, the modified model equations read [cf. Eqs. (3.16)]:

$$\frac{du_{ij}}{dt} = \frac{1}{\epsilon}[u_{ij}(1-u_{ij})(u_{ij}-a) - v_{ij} + d] + D_u J_{ij}, \quad (7.1)$$
$$\frac{dv_{ij}}{dt} = u_{ij} - c_{ij}v_{ij} + e_{ij} + \xi_{ij}(t) + A\cos(\omega t),$$

where A denotes the amplitude and ω the frequency of the external signal. Both parameters are fixed throughout this chapter ($A = 0.04$, $\omega = 0.6$ $t.u.^{-1}$). For the given value of ω, the period of the external signal is large compared to internal time scales. In this section, the symmetric bistable regime is considered and the multiplicative variability is neglected ($\sigma_{v,c} = 0.0$, $c_{ij} = c = 6.7$). Furthermore, no multiplicative noise is applied throughout this and the following sections. To save computational time, the net size is reduced to $N = 100$. For larger nets, the results are even quantitatively the same.

For the given set of parameters and without variability and noise, the signal can not induce jumps between the two stable states. The net remains in one of the stable fixed points. To quantify the response of the net to the external signal, the linear response Q [Eq. (4.18)] is used. In Fig. 7.7, Q is plotted in dependency on $\sigma_{v,e}$ and $\sigma_{n,e}$ for a globally

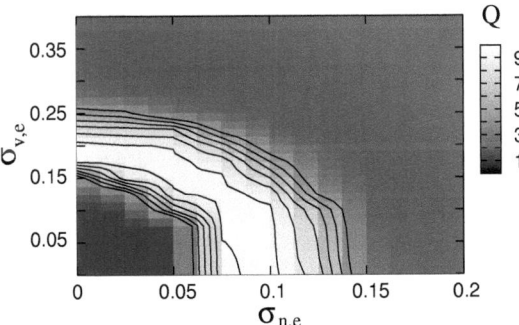

Figure 7.7: *Linear response Q [Eq. (4.18)] for a globally coupled net of FHN elements [Eqs. (7.1)] dependent on the strengths of additive variability $\sigma_{v,e}$ and additive noise $\sigma_{n,e}$. Contour lines from the outside to the inside: $Q = 4.5, 5.5, 6.5, 7.5, 8.5, 9.5$. Further parameters: Parameter set 2, $c = 6.7$ (symmetric bistable regime), $E = -0.2$, $N = 100$, $D_u = 20$, $A = 0.04$, $\omega = 0.6$ $t.u.^{-1}$, $\sigma_{n,c} = 0.0$, $\sigma_{v,c} = 0.0$ [23].*

coupled net. The linear response Q shows a resonance-like behavior due to both, additive variability and additive noise. Without noise ($\sigma_{n,e} = 0.0$), the signal is optimally enhanced for intermediate values of $\sigma_{v,e}$ (*diversity-induced resonance* [21, 23]). Without variability ($\sigma_{v,e} = 0.0$), the system shows the well-known phenomenon of *stochastic resonance*, where the optimal signal enhancement is reached at intermediate noise strengths $\sigma_{n,e}$ [14]. The symmetry of the linear response with respect to $\sigma_{v,e}$ and $\sigma_{n,e}$ is exhibited in Fig. 7.7 and shows that one can replace additive noise by additive variability. The more noise is present, the less variability is necessary to achieve optimal signal enhancement and vice versa.

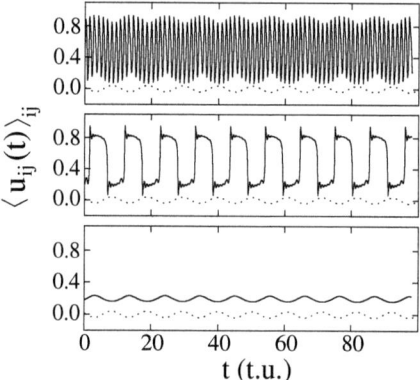

Figure 7.8: *Time series of the mean field $\langle u_{ij}(t)\rangle_{ij}$ of a globally coupled net of FHN elements [Eqs. (7.1)] for different strengths of the additive variability. From bottom to top: $\sigma_{v,e} = 0.1, 0.2, 0.3$. (—) $\langle u_{ij}(t)\rangle_{ij}$, (− · · −) the external signal. Further parameters: Parameter set 2, $c = 6.7$ (symmetric bistable regime), $E = -0.2$, $N = 100$, $D_u = 20$, $A = 0.04$, $\omega = 0.6\, t.u.^{-1}$, $\sigma_{n,c} = 0.0$, $\sigma_{v,c} = 0.0$, $\sigma_{n,e} = 0.0$ [23].*

Without additive noise, the temporal evolution of the net is deterministic. Additive variability causes a shift of the linear nullcline for each element [Fig. 7.1 (b)]. The distribution of parameter e_{ij} is shown in Fig. 7.3 (b). For $\sigma_{v,e} > 0$, there are bistable elements, which are driven beyond the threshold of one of its fixed points by the external signal, and even excitable elements (regimes $E1$ and $\tilde{E}1$). The bistable elements may switch to the other stable state, if they are uncoupled. In Fig. 7.8, time series of the mean field of $u_{ij}(t)$ are plotted for different values of $\sigma_{v,e}$. For a small variability strength (e.g. $\sigma_{v,e} = 0.1$), the signal can not induce jumps between the two stable states for most of the elements. So due to the coupling, the net remains in one of the two stable fixed points. Increasing the variability strength $\sigma_{v,e}$, more and more elements can switch to the other stable state at a certain phase of the external signal. These elements pull the others producing a collective behavior. The whole net is performing jumps between the two stable states synchronized to the external forcing (Fig. 7.8, $\sigma_{v,e} = 0.2$). For an even larger variability strength (e.g. $\sigma_{v,e} = 0.3$), the net permanently jumps between the two stable states, like a synchronized oscillation, but independent of the phase of the external signal. The signal is not enhanced in the response of the net anymore. The permanent jumps of the net between the two stable states can also be observed without an external signal at a certain level of additive variability or noise. For very large variability strengths, the collective behavior gets more and more lost. The response of a net of bistable FHN elements to a weak external signal

7.4. DOUBLY VARIABILITY-INDUCED RESONANCE

shows a resonance-like dependency on the strength of additive variability. This result confirms that the phenomenon of *diversity-induced resonance* might occur in many spatially extended systems [21, 23].

The corresponding time series of the mean field of $u_{ij}(t)$ dependent on $\sigma_{n,e}$ without variability show the same behavior as those in Fig. 7.8. Replacing additive noise by additive variability leads in this case to a very similar collective behavior.

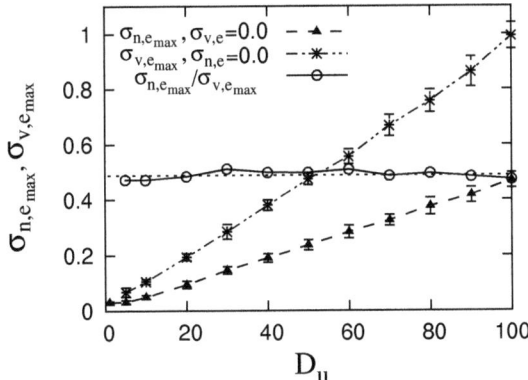

Figure 7.9: $\sigma_{n,e_{max}}$, $\sigma_{v,e_{max}}$, and their quotient dependent on the coupling strength D_u. (···) The mean value of the quotients $\langle \sigma_{n,e_{max}}/\sigma_{v,e_{max}} \rangle = 0.49$. Further parameters: Parameter set 2, $c = 6.7$ (symmetric bistable regime), $E = -0.2$, $N = 100$, $A = 0.04$, $\omega = 0.6$ t.u.$^{-1}$, $\sigma_{n,c} = 0.0$, $\sigma_{v,c} = 0.0$ [23].

The observed resonance strongly depends on the coupling strength. The value of $\sigma_{v,e}$ for $\sigma_{n,e} = 0.0$ and $\sigma_{n,e}$ for $\sigma_{v,e} = 0.0$, at which Q takes its maximum, are denoted as $\sigma_{v,e_{max}}$ and $\sigma_{n,e_{max}}$, respectively. Both $\sigma_{v,e_{max}}$ and $\sigma_{n,e_{max}}$ linearly depend on the coupling strength over a wide range of D_u (Fig. 7.9). Their quotient is approximately a constant ($\sigma_{n,e_{max}}/\sigma_{v,e_{max}} \approx 0.49$). So one needs roughly for additive variability twice the strength compared to additive noise to get optimal signal enhancement for the investigated range of D_u. For vanishing coupling strength, $\sigma_{n,e_{max}}$ tends to 0.04, the value one gets for a single uncoupled element. Regarding additive variability, the response of the net shows no resonance for $D_u < 5$. So a minimum coupling strength is essential to obtain diversity-induced resonance.

7.4 Doubly Variability-Induced Resonance

Now the combined influence of multiplicative variability and additive variability on the response of the net to the external signal is investigated. The simulations are performed without additive and multiplicative noise ($\sigma_{n,e} = 0.0$, $\sigma_{n,c} = 0.0$) starting in the asymmetric bistable regime ($C = 7.3$). In Fig. 7.10, the linear response Q [Eq. (4.18)] of a globally

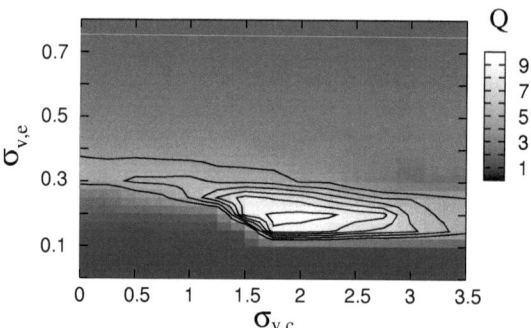

Figure 7.10: *Linear response Q [Eq. (4.18)] for a globally coupled net of FHN elements [Eqs. (7.1)] dependent on the strengths of additive $\sigma_{v,e}$ and multiplicative variability $\sigma_{v,c}$. Contour lines as in Fig. 7.7. Further parameters: Parameter set 2, $C = 7.3$, $E = -0.2$, $N = 100$, $D_u = 20$, $A = 0.04$, $\omega = 0.6$ t.u.$^{-1}$, $\sigma_{n,c} = 0.0$, $\sigma_{n,e} = 0.0$ [23].*

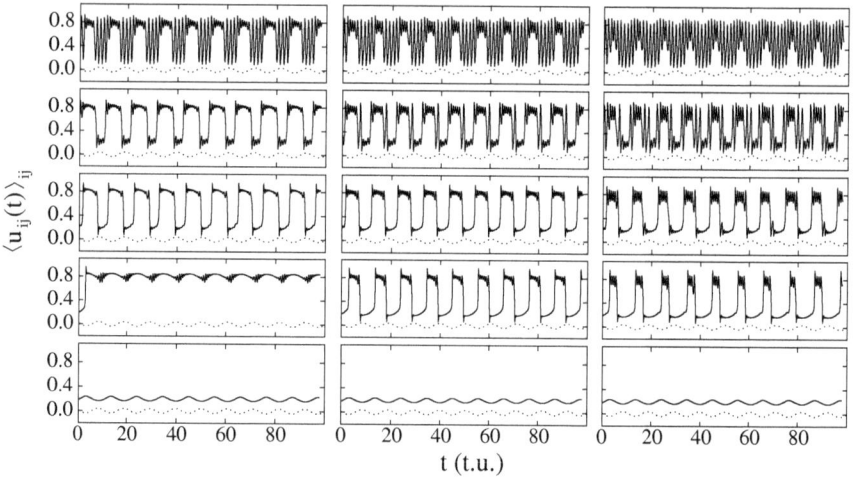

Figure 7.11: *Time series of the mean field $\langle u_{ij}(t)\rangle_{ij}$ of a globally coupled net of FHN elements [Eqs. (7.1)] for different strengths of $\sigma_{v,c}$ and $\sigma_{v,e}$. Left column: $\sigma_{v,c} = 1.5$. Middle column: $\sigma_{v,c} = 2.0$. Right column: $\sigma_{v,c} = 2.5$. In each column from bottom to top: $\sigma_{v,e} = 0.1, 0.15, 0.2, 0.25, 0.3$. (—) $\langle u_{ij}(t)\rangle_{ij}$, (— · · —) the external signal. Further parameters: Parameter set 2, $C = 7.3$, $E = -0.2$, $N = 100$, $D_u = 20$, $A = 0.04$, $\omega = 0.6$ t.u.$^{-1}$, $\sigma_{n,c} = 0.0$, $\sigma_{n,e} = 0.0$ [23].*

7.4. DOUBLY VARIABILITY-INDUCED RESONANCE

coupled net is shown in dependency on $\sigma_{v,e}$ and $\sigma_{v,c}$. The additive variability is responsible for the hopping between the two stable states synchronized to the external signal (see section 7.3). This also works in the asymmetric bistable regime ($C = 7.3$ and $\sigma_{v,c} = 0.0$), but the maximum of Q is shifted to larger values of $\sigma_{v,e}$ and it is less pronounced.

Applying additionally multiplicative variability, the maximum is reached for smaller values of $\sigma_{v,e}$ and is more pronounced. For an optimal value of $\sigma_{v,c} \approx 2.0$, the linear response curve takes its absolute maximum value. For even larger values of $\sigma_{v,c}$, the maximum of the resonance curve decreases again. As shown in section 7.2, the multiplicative variability changes the mean threshold for a transition from the upper to the lower stable fixed point. Thus due to the systematic influence of the multiplicative variability, a transition towards the symmetric bistable regime is induced, which is reach for $\sigma_{v,c} \approx 2.0$ [cf. Fig. 7.4 (e)]. So via symmetry restoration by multiplicative variability, the response of the net to the signal is further enhanced. This effect is called *doubly diversity-induced resonance* [23], because both, additive and multiplicative variability, are necessary to enhance the external signal optimally.

To manifest this result, time series of the mean field of $u_{ij}(t)$ are plotted for particular values of $\sigma_{v,e}$ and $\sigma_{v,c}$ in Fig. 7.11. In each column (different fixed values of $\sigma_{v,c}$) one sees that the additive variability is responsible for the hopping between the two stable states synchronized to the external signal, as described in the previous section for the symmetric bistable regime (see section 7.3). The strength of additive variability, at which the external signal is optimally enhanced in the response of the net, depends on the value of $\sigma_{v,c}$. The systematic influence of the multiplicative variability causes a modification of the mean thresholds for the transitions between the two stable fixed points. Comparing the time series for $\sigma_{v,e} = 0.2$ of Fig. 7.11, one discerns that for $\sigma_{v,c} = 2.0$ the symmetric bistable regime is induced. The thresholds for a transition and the inverse transition between the two stable states are approximately of the same size. The net spends the same time in each of the stable states between two consecutive jumps.

In Figs. 7.12 and 7.13, respectively, the results of the simulations for diffusively coupled nets are shown. The linear response Q shows again a well-pronounced maximum in dependency on $\sigma_{v,e}$ and $\sigma_{v,c}$ (Fig. 7.12). In comparison to the globally coupled case (Fig. 7.10), the optimal signal enhancement is reached for a slightly smaller value of the multiplicative variability strength ($\sigma_{v,c} = 1.75$). Regarding the influence of additive variability, the optimal signal enhancement occurs approximately at the same values of $\sigma_{v,e}$ compared to the globally coupled case. But the decrease of Q beyond the optimal signal enhancement is stretched over a larger range of $\sigma_{v,e}$. In Fig. 7.13, time series of the mean field of $u_{ij}(t)$ are shown for particular values of $\sigma_{v,e}$ and for the optimal value of $\sigma_{v,c}$ ($\sigma_{v,c} = 1.75$). Analogous to the results of the globally coupled net, the additive variability is responsible for the hopping between the two stable states synchronized to the external signal and the multiplicative variability induces the symmetry. In a diffusively coupled net, the elements, which can switch to the other stable state at a certain phase of the signal, pull their nearest-neighbor elements to the other stable state. So a jump from one stable state to the other propagates like a phase wave through the whole net in contrast to the globally coupled net. That is the reason, why the time series of the mean field are smoother compared to the globally coupled case.

An obvious difference to the globally coupled case is that an increase of the strength

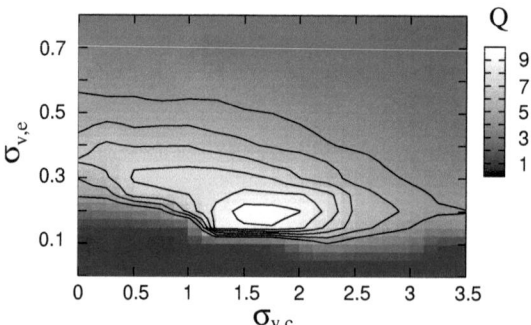

Figure 7.12: *Linear response Q [Eq. (4.18)] for a diffusively coupled net of FHN elements [Eqs. (7.1)] dependent on the strengths of additive $\sigma_{v,e}$ and multiplicative variability $\sigma_{v,c}$. Contour lines as in Fig. 7.7. Further parameters: Parameter set 2, $C = 7.3$, $E = -0.2$, $N = 100$, $D_u = 20$, $A = 0.04$, $\omega = 0.6$ t.u.$^{-1}$, $\sigma_{n,c} = 0.0$, $\sigma_{n,e} = 0.0$ [23].*

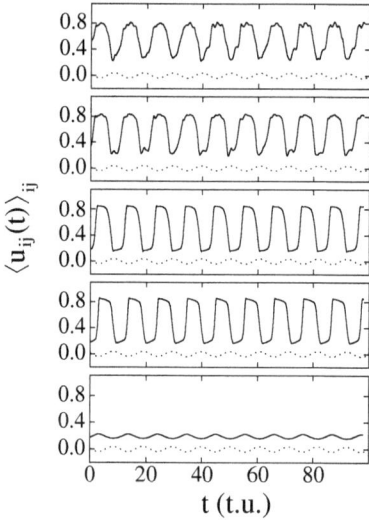

Figure 7.13: *Time series of the mean field $\langle u_{ij}(t) \rangle_{ij}$ of a diffusively coupled net of FHN elements [Eqs. (7.1)] for different strengths of $\sigma_{v,e}$. From bottom to top: $\sigma_{v,e} = 0.1, 0.15, 0.2, 0.25, 0.3$. (—) $\langle u_{ij}(t) \rangle_{ij}$, (– · · –) the external signal. Further parameters: Parameter set 2, $C = 7.3$, $E = -0.2$, $N = 100$, $D_u = 20$, $A = 0.04$, $\omega = 0.6$ t.u.$^{-1}$, $\sigma_{n,c} = 0.0$, $\sigma_{n,e} = 0.0$, $\sigma_{v,c} = 1.75$ [23].*

of additive variability beyond the optimal value does not induce the oscillation-like permanent hopping between the two stable states. The global coupling forces all elements to act synchronously and leads thereby to the oscillation-like permanent hopping, which is responsible for the fast decrease of Q at large values of $\sigma_{v,e}$. The diffusive coupling can not force all elements to act synchronously at large values of $\sigma_{v,e}$, only ever smaller clusters jump synchronously. That is the reason, why the collective behavior monotonously disappears with higher values of $\sigma_{v,e}$. The amplitude of the mean-field time series gets smaller, and the external signal becomes less and less enhanced in the response of the net over a wide range of $\sigma_{v,e}$.

The maximum values of the response Q are approximately the same for the globally (Fig. 7.10) and the diffusively coupled net (Fig. 7.12). The amplitude of the response of the net is determined by the positions of the two stable states, which is the same in both cases independent of the type of coupling. And the time for a jump from one stable state to the other is very short compared to the period of the signal for diffusive and global coupling. For that reason, there is no noticeable difference between the maximum values of the response of the globally and the diffusively coupled net. In comparison to the maximum value of the response of the net in the symmetric bistable regime (Fig. 7.7), one sees again no considerable difference. This underlines that the symmetric bistable regime is induced for intermediate values of the multiplicative variability strength.

7.5 Influence of Time-Delayed Feedback on Bistable FitzHugh-Nagumo Elements

In this section, a brief outlook is given about the influence of time-delayed feedback on the dynamics of bistable FHN elements, where further investigations might follow in the future. Considering an overdamped particle in a double-wall potential, first investigations on bistable dynamics with feedback control have been done [86]. It was shown that time-delayed feedback influences both the coherence resonance effect and the stochastic resonance effect. Also in excitable and oscillatory systems, the influence of time-delayed feedback on coherence resonance and stochastic resonance has been studied [87, 88]. Here the influence of time-delayed feedback on the stochastic resonance effect of a single FHN element and a net of FHN elements is studied. Only local feedback in the variable $v(t)$ is considered. Hence, the model equations with additive noise and external signal in the slow variable $v(t)$ read

$$\frac{du_{ij}}{dt} = \frac{1}{\epsilon}[u_{ij}(1-u_{ij})(u_{ij}-a) - v_{ij} + d] + D_u J_{ij}\,,$$
$$\frac{dv_{ij}}{dt} = u_{ij} - cv_{ij} + e + \xi_{ij}(t) + K[v_{ij}(t-\tau) - v_{ij}(t)] + A\cos(\omega t)\,. \tag{7.2}$$

As in the previous sections, the amplitude and the frequency of the external signal are fixed at $A = 0.04$ and $\omega = 0.6\ t.u.^{-1}$, respectively. In this section, no multiplicative noise and no variability are present. The parameter values of c and e are fixed at $c = 6.7$ and $e = -0.2$ for all elements. Thus, the elements are in the symmetric bistable regime. To induce jumps between the two stable states, additive noise is used.

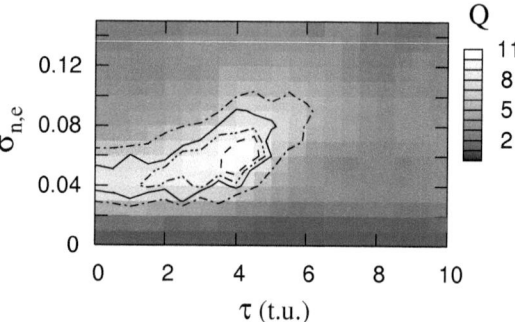

Figure 7.14: *Linear response Q [Eq. (4.18)] for a single uncoupled FHN element with local feedback in v(t) [Eqs. (7.2)] dependent on the strength of additive noise $\sigma_{n,e}$ and on the delay time τ. Contour lines: (− · −) Q = 7.0; (—) Q = 8.0; (− ··−) Q = 9.0; (− − −) Q = 10.0. Further parameters: Parameter set 2, c = 6.7, e = −0.2, N = 1, A = 0.04, $\omega = 0.6\, t.u.^{-1}$, K = 1.0, $g_f = 1.0$.*

First the dynamics of a single element is investigated. In Fig. 7.14, the linear response Q [Eq. (4.18)] of a single uncoupled FHN element is plotted dependent on the noise strength $\sigma_{n,e}$ and the delay time τ. The feedback strength is fixed at $K = 1.0$, a value, for which the feedback has a reasonable influence on the system dynamics. For $\tau = 0.0\, t.u.$, the feedback signal vanishes and the element shows the well-known stochastic resonance effect. The linear response Q is maximal ($Q \approx 8$) for intermediate noise strengths. Increasing the delay time τ, the stochastic resonance peak is even more pronounced. The maximum value of Q slightly increases until $\tau \approx 4.5\, t.u.$ For e.g. $\tau = 4.0\, t.u.$, the enhancement of the signal is about 30% larger ($Q = 10.6$). Then, for larger values of τ ($\tau > 4.5\, t.u.$), the maximum of Q decreases quickly, no stochastic resonance effect is found anymore for $\tau > 6.5\, t.u.$

To explain the influence of the feedback on the stochastic resonance effect, time series of a single element without external signal are studied [Figs. 7.15 (a)-(c)]. Weak additive noise ($\sigma_{n,e} = 0.03$) randomly induces transitions between the two stable fixed points. If no feedback is applied [Fig. 7.15 (a)], the element remains for an arbitrary time in one of the stable fixed points between two consecutive jumps. The residence time in one of the stable fixed points ranges from $0.5\, t.u.$ up to $12\, t.u.$ and longer. With feedback ($K = 1.0$), irrespective of a transient no short residence times are found [Figs. 7.15 (b) and 7.15 (c)]. Particularly, for $\tau = 4.0\, t.u.$ [Fig. 7.15 (b)] all residence times are longer than $4.0\, t.u.$ and for $\tau = 8.0\, t.u.$ [Fig. 7.15 (c)] all residence times are longer than $8.0\, t.u.$ Due to the time-delayed feedback, the threshold for a transition from one stable state to the other is enlarged. When the element remains in one of the stable fixed points at time $t - \tau$, the model equations can be rewritten by introducing the effective parameters $c_{tdf} = c + K$ and $e_{tdf} = e + Kv_{st}$ ($c = 6.7$, $e = -0.2$), just like in section 6.1.1. This leads to new effective linear nullclines [Fig. 7.15 (d)], which determine the dynamics of the FHN element. Three

7.5. INFLUENCE OF TIME-DELAYED FEEDBACK

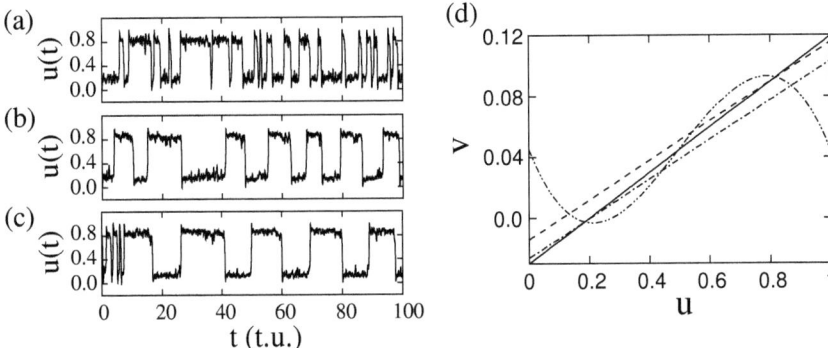

Figure 7.15: *(a)-(c) Time series of a single uncoupled FHN element with feedback in $v(t)$ [Eqs. (7.2)], driven by additive noise ($\sigma_{n,e} = 0.03$), and without external signal ($A = 0.0$) for three different values of τ. (a) $\tau = 0.0\,t.u.$, (b) $\tau = 4.0\,t.u.$, (c) $\tau = 8.0\,t.u.$ (d) Nullclines of a bistable FHN element with feedback in $v(t)$. (—··—) Cubic nullcline, (——) linear nullcline for a vanishing feedback signal, (— — —) and (— · —) effective linear nullclines, when the delayed state and the current state are unequal (see text for further explanations). Further parameters: Parameter set 2, $c = 6.7$, $e = -0.2$, $N = 1$, $K = 1$, $g_f = 1.0$.*

cases have to be differentiated. If the element remains at time t and at time $t - \tau$ in the same stable fixed point, the feedback signal vanishes and the thresholds for transitions between the two stable fixed points persist unchanged [Fig. 7.15 (d)]. If the element remains at time t in the lower stable fixed point and at time $t - \tau$ in the upper one, the effective parameters are $c_{tdf} = 6.7 + 1.0 = 7.7$ and $e_{tdf} = -0.2 + 1.0 * 0.092 = -0.108$, and the threshold for a transition back to the upper stable fixed point is strongly increased [Fig. 7.15 (d)]. And if the element remains at time t in the upper stable fixed point and at time $t - \tau$ in the lower one, the effective parameters are $c_{tdf} = 6.7 + 1.0 = 7.7$ and $e_{tdf} = -0.2 + 1.0 * (-0.002) = -0.202$, and the threshold for a transition back to the lower stable fixed point is strongly increased [Fig. 7.15 (d)]. This explains why for moderate noise strengths no jumps between the two stable states occur for residence times smaller than τ, if feedback is applied.

For the stochastic resonance effect, this means that besides the external signal a second characteristic time scale is given by the time-delayed feedback. In the case of resonance, the frequency of the signal determines the time between two consecutive jumps, which is about $5.2\,t.u.$ Since a transition between the two stable fixed points lasts about $0.5\,t.u.$, the time that the element optimally rests in one of the stable states comes up to $4.7\,t.u.$ As shown above, after a transition to the other stable state the time-delayed feedback suppresses the backward transition for the following time span of τ. This explains why the external signal is optimally enhanced in the response of the element for a range of the delay time of $3.6\,t.u. < \tau < 4.7\,t.u.$ Here the two time scales match perfectly and thus the value of Q is maximal. Increasing the value of τ from $0.0\,t.u.$ to $4.7\,t.u.$, the time span, where additional transitions between the to stable states are suppressed, becomes longer and longer. And thus the value of Q slightly increases until the optimal τ-value of $\tau = 4.7$. For larger values of τ, the stochastic resonance effect disappears quickly, because the feedback suppresses a transition even when the external signal wants to kick the element into the other stable state. Thus, the frequency of the signal is not represented in the response of the element anymore.

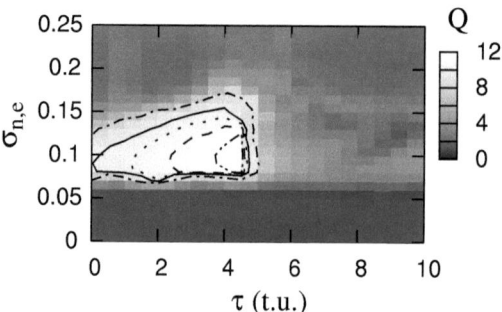

Figure 7.16: *Linear response Q [Eq. (4.18)] for a globally coupled net of FHN elements with local feedback in $v(t)$ [Eqs. (7.2)] dependent on the strength of additive noise $\sigma_{n,e}$ and on the delay time τ. Contour lines: $(-\cdot -)$ $Q = 9.5$; $(—)$ $Q = 10.0$; $(\cdots)$ $Q = 10.5$; $(- - -)$ $Q = 11.0$; $(-\cdot\cdot -)$ $Q = 11.5$. Further parameters: Parameter set 2, $c = 6.7$, $e = -0.2$, $N = 100$, $D_u = 20$, $A = 0.04$, $\omega = 0.6\,t.u.^{-1}$, $K = 1.0$, $g_f = 1.0$.*

In a next step, the response of a globally coupled net to the external signal under the influence of time-delayed feedback is investigated. The feedback strength K is again equal to 1.0, and all elements get the feedback signal ($g_f = 1.0$). In Fig. 7.16, the linear response Q of a globally coupled net is plotted dependent on the delay time τ and the noise strength $\sigma_{n,e}$. Similar to the result of a single element [cf. 7.14], the linear response Q exhibits a pronounced resonance peak for intermediate values of τ and $\sigma_{n,e}$. As larger the value of τ ($0.0\,t.u. < \tau < 4.7\,t.u.$), the longer the time span is, where additional transitions between the two stable states are suppressed due to the feedback. This results in the larger value of Q. And just like for the single element, the stochastic resonance effect disappears quickly for $\tau > 4.7\,t.u.$ The explanation is the same as for the single element.

Whereas without feedback, the maximal value of the linear response is approximately $Q = 9.8$, with feedback this value is about 20% larger ($Q \approx 11.7$). Thus, the response of a net of bistable elements to a weak external signal driven by additive noise, can be further enhanced via time-delayed feedback. This result is also found for diffusively coupled nets. More investigations to the influence of time-delayed feedback on the stochastic resonance effect and on the diversity-induced resonance effect in spatially extended systems might follow in future. For example, the impact of global feedback should be studied. Further open questions are the influence of the quota g_f of elements that get the feedback signal

7.5. INFLUENCE OF TIME-DELAYED FEEDBACK

or the influence of the spatial correlation of the controlled elements on the stochastic (or diversity-induced) resonance effect.

Summarizing, in this chapter it is shown that multiplicative variability systematically can change the dynamics of a net of bistable FHN elements. Considering a weak external signal, the response of the net is optimal for intermediate values of the additive and the multiplicative variability strength (doubly variability-induced resonance). Moreover, the response of the net to the external signal can further be enhanced applying time-delayed feedback with appropriately chosen delay times.

Chapter 8
Summary and Outlook

In this thesis, the influence of noise, variability, and time-delayed feedback on the dynamics of nets of neural elements is investigated. After a brief introduction and motivation, the characteristics of the stochastic terms (noise and variability) and the types of feedback control are introduced in chapter 2. The model systems under consideration are nets of FitzHugh-Nagumo and Hodgkin-Huxley elements, respectively. The model equations and their dynamics are discussed in chapter 3. The FitzHugh-Nagumo model is suitable for the study of general dynamical properties, because it is a minimal model that exhibits excitable, oscillatory and bistable dynamics. The results, which are found for excitable and oscillatory nets of FitzHugh-Nagumo elements, are verified using the Hodgkin-Huxley model, the first phenomenological model of neuronal activity derived to fit experimental data. Thus, these results might play a role in real neural networks. In chapter 4, theoretical approaches to estimate the influence of multiplicative noise and multiplicative variability are introduced. And besides that, in this chapter a couple of quantities, which may serve as order parameters to discern the different dynamical features, are presented. After these introducing chapters, in the next three chapters the results are displayed.

In chapter 5, the influence of time-delayed feedback control on oscillatory neural dynamics is investigated. First, the dynamics of a single FitzHugh-Nagumo element is studied. It is shown that via time-delayed feedback control the former unstable fixed point, which is surrounded by a stable limit cycle, can be stabilized. For appropriately chosen values of the feedback parameters, the element rests in the fixed point instead of performing autonomous limit cycle oscillations. This effect is called amplitude death, since the amplitude of the oscillation tends to zero. The amplitude death regime can be predicted very well by a linear stability analysis. Due to the feedback term, one gets a transcendental characteristic equation, whose eigenvalues can be calculated numerically. Besides the amplitude death regime, a region is found where the stable focus and a stable limit cycle coexist. In the amplitude death regime, the single element is excitable. Applying weak additive noise, the element shows the typical spiking behavior of excitable neural dynamics. Thus, due to the feedback, the oscillation is suppressed and excitable behavior is induced.

Then, nets of FitzHugh-Nagumo elements are studied, which perform global oscillations in the absence of feedback. With feedback, the amplitude death regime is found for two types of time-delayed feedback (local and global feedback). In the amplitude death regime, additional noise excites wave fronts, which propagate through the whole net (excitable behavior). Thus due to the feedback, the global oscillation is suppressed and excitable net dynamics is induced, which allows for signal transmission (excitation waves).

Regarding a net, also the influence of the quota of elements that get the feedback signal on the amplitude death regime is investigated. It is shown that for appropriate values of the feedback parameters, it is sufficient to control only 20% of all elements to ensure that the whole net remains in the stabilized fixed point. Furthermore, the influence of clustered control (spatial correlation of the controlled elements) on the amplitude death regime is studied. Here only half of the elements get the feedback signal. If the correlation length is too large, within the clusters without feedback some elements can not be forced to become stabilized fixed points and oscillate. These elements excite their neighboring elements and wave fronts propagate through the whole net. No amplitude death regime is found anymore. Finally, the influence of the coupling strength on the amplitude death regime is investigated. Amplitude death is found for a large range of coupling strengths, but a minimum coupling strength is necessary to observe this collective effect, if only a certain quota of the elements gets the feedback signal. All results, presented for the FitzHugh-Nagumo model in section 5.1, are confirmed using the more realistic and complex Hodgkin-Huxley model (see section 5.2).

Generally, these results confirm that time-delayed feedback control provides an efficient method to achieve a qualitative change of the dynamics of spatially extended systems. Due to feedback, global oscillations are suppressed and excitable behavior is induced.

In chapter 6, the influence of time-delayed feedback on pattern formation in subexcitable nets is studied. Without feedback, all excitations die out after a quite short propagation length due to the subexcitability of the net. It is shown that with feedback the excitation waves can grow and spread out through the whole net. Thus for appropriate values of the feedback parameters, the feedback sustains pattern formation. This effect is studied in detail for wave fronts, which are either induced by special initial conditions, by noise, or by variability. For wave fronts induced by special initial conditions and noise-induced wave fronts, pattern formation is sustained for a large range of the delay time. The noise-induced patterns are most coherent for intermediate values of the delay time. Connected with the coherence of the patterns, the amount of the transmitted information (number of wave fronts) shows a resonance-like dependency on the delay time. For variability-induced wave fronts ranges of the delay time, where coherent pattern formation is sustained, alternate with ranges of the delay time, where the formation of any excitations is suppressed. In the case of variability-induced patterns, clusters of oscillating elements act as excitation centers. Since for values of the delay time around half the oscillation period, some oscillatory elements are in the amplitude death regime, there no patterns are found and all elements rest in the fixed point.

Besides the feedback strength and the delay time, the quota of elements that get the feedback signal is varied. It is shown that it is sufficient to control about 40% of all elements to reach excitable behavior. Furthermore, again the influence of clustered control is studied, where only half of the elements get the feedback signal. It is shown that clustered control favors the propagation of excitation waves. For wave fronts induced by special initial conditions, the results are confirmed using the Hodgkin-Huxley model.

The results presented underline that time-delayed feedback may have a crucial influence on the dynamics of spatially extended nonlinear systems, especially on pattern forming processes. In particular, the interaction of feedback and noise, which leads to most coherent moving patterns (maximal amount of transmitted information) for an intermediate delay time, might be of interest for many systems in which information transport is of importance.

The influence of noise and variability on a net of bistable FitzHugh-Nagumo elements is investigated in chapter 7. After a short introduction of the bistable dynamics of a single element, the influence of multiplicative noise and multiplicative variability on the dynamics of nets is discussed. Starting in the asymmetric bistable regime (thresholds for a transition from one stable fixed point to the other and for the inverse transition are unequal), it is shown that the multiplicative stochastic terms can induce the symmetric bistable regime (equal thresholds for the transitions). This systematic influence of the multiplicative stochastic terms can be explained quite well by theoretical approaches, which are introduced in chapter 4. Particularly, the small noise expansion yields a good prediction of the net dynamics.

Then, the response of a net to a weak, external, periodic signal is studied. First, the elements are in the symmetric bistable regime and only additive stochastic terms are considered. Due to additive noise, the net shows the well-known stochastic resonance effect. Applying additive variability only, the net exhibits also a resonant behavior. For intermediate values of the additive variability strength, the external signal is optimally enhanced in the response of the net (diversity-induced resonance). The more noise is present, the less variability is necessary to achieve optimal signal enhancement and vice versa. Thus, one can replace noise by variability regarding the enhancement of the external signal. In a next step, additive and multiplicative variability are applied, where the net is in the asymmetric bistable regime. It is shown that the response of the net to the external signal is optimally for intermediate values of both, the additive and the multiplicative variability strength (doubly diversity-induced resonance). The additive variability induces the hopping between the two stable states synchronized to the external signal, and the multiplicative variability induces the symmetric bistable regime, where the response is optimal. This result is found for globally and diffusively coupled nets.

In the end of chapter 7, the influence of time-delayed feedback on the stochastic resonance effect of a single bistable element and of nets of bistable elements is discussed. It is shown that the response to the external signal can further be enhanced, if feedback with appropriately chosen parameter values is applied. The optimal response is attained if the delay time matches to half of the period of the external signal.

The findings presented may contribute to a theoretical understanding of the dynamics of spatially extended, nonlinear systems under the influence of noise, variability, and time-delayed feedback. Time-delayed feedback control provides an efficient method to manipulate the dynamics of a system in a desired manner. Controlling pattern forming processes or stochastic resonance effects might be of importance for many applications in several fields of physics, neuroscience, and biology. Regarding some medical applications, the time-delayed feedback control provides a strategy to suppress neuronal malfunctions. For example in neuronal diseases, like Parkinson's disease, epilepsy, and tremor, the movement disorders of a patient are connected with synchronized oscillations of neurons in the brain. As shown in this thesis, time-delayed feedback control can suppress globally synchronized oscillations and induce excitable behavior. Hopefully, these findings may help to develop new clinical approaches to suppress such neuronal malfunctions. A medical application, where the propagation of excitation waves plays a crucial role, is the occurrence of migraine. Maybe the results presented help to find a solution to suppress attacks of migraine in a sustainable way.

In this context, it is desirable that more realistic models, which are fitted to the specific disease, are developed and investigated. Generally, a number of investigations might follow discussing the influence of other feedback types on the dynamics of spatially extended systems. The interplay of stochastic forces and time-delayed feedback on pattern forming processes provides many open questions. Hopefully, this work does also foster experimental investigations to obtain realistic models and may in the end contribute to successful applications, especially regarding neural diseases.

Zusammenfassung

In der vorliegenden Arbeit wird der Einfluss von Rauschen, Variabilität und zeitverzögerter Rückkopplungskontrolle auf die Dynamik von Netzwerken aus neuronalen Elementen untersucht. Die Dynamik der einzelnen Elemente wird durch die FitzHugh-Nagumo-, die Hodgkin-Huxley- oder die reduzierten Hodgkin-Huxley-Gleichungen beschrieben. Nach einer kurzen Einführung und Motivation, werden in Kapitel 2 die Eigenschaften der Rausch- und Variabilitätsterme erklärt und die zwei verwendeten Rückkopplungsarten eingeführt. In Kapitel 3 werden die Modellgleichungen und ihre Dynamik diskutiert. Alle Modelle zeigen anregbares (exzitatorisches) und oszillierendes Verhalten. Das FitzHugh-Nagumo-Modell kann darüber hinaus auch bistabil sein. In Kapitel 4 werden theoretische Näherungen, die den Einfluss von Rauschen und Variabilität auf die Netzwerkdynamik beschreiben, erläutert. Außerdem werden einige Größen eingeführt, die dazu dienen, die Netzwerkdynamik zu klassifizieren und zu quantifizieren. Nach diesen einleitenden Kapiteln folgt in den nächsten drei Kapiteln die Präsentation der Ergebnisse.

In Kapitel 5 wird der Einfluss von zeitverzögerter Rückkopplungskontrolle auf oszillierende neuronale Elemente (FitzHugh-Nagumo- und Hodgkin-Huxley-Modelle) untersucht. Sowohl für einzelne Elemente als auch für Netze findet man den sogenannten Amplitudentod der Oszillation für beide Rückkopplungsarten. Aufgrund der Rückkopplung wird der eigentlich instabile Fokus, der von einem stabilen Grenzzyklus umgeben ist, für geeignet gewählte Parameterwerte der Verzögerungszeit und der Rückkopplungsstärke stabilisiert. Das einzelne Element beziehungsweise alle Elemente eines Netzes ruhen im stabilisierten Fixpunkt. In diesem dynamischen Gebiet zeigt das einzelne Element wie auch das Netz exzitatorisches Verhalten. Additives Rauschen regt einzelne Pulse beziehungsweise Wellen an, die sich durch das ganze Netz ausbreiten. Geeignete Rückkopplung kann also Oszillationen unterdrücken und exzitatorisches Verhalten, welches Signalübermittlung in Form von Anregungswellen unterstützt, induzieren. Das Ergebnis einer linearen Stabilitätsanalyse der Modellgleichungen mit Rückkopplungsterm stimmt sehr gut mit den numerischen Simulationen überein. Für Netze wird des Weiteren die Abhängigkeit der Dynamik von der Anzahl der Elemente, die das Rückkopplungssignal bekommen, und von deren Korrelation untersucht. Es kann ausreichend sein, 20% aller Elemente per Rückkopplung zu kontrollieren, um zu erreichen, dass das gesamte Netz im stabilisierten Fixpunkt ruht. Dies ist allerdings nur möglich, wenn die Elemente, die das Rückkopplungssignal bekommen, nahezu unkorreliert sind. Zusätzlich wird der Einfluss der Kopplungsstärke zwischen den Elementen auf die Netzdynamik studiert. Es wird gezeigt, dass der Amplitudentod für einen großen Bereich an Kopplungsstärken auftritt, man aber eine bestimmte Kopplungsstärke braucht, um diesen kollektiven Effekt zu beobachten, falls nur ein Teil der Elemente über das Rückkopplungssignal kontrolliert wird.

Diese Ergebnisse zeigen, dass durch geeignete Rückkopplungskontrolle die Dynamik eines räumlich ausgedehnten Systems grundlegend verändert wird. Zeitverzögerte Rückkopplung kann Oszillationen in neuronalen Netzen unterdrücken und exzitatorische Dynamik induzieren.

In Kapitel 6 wird der Einfluss von zeitverzögerter Rückkopplungskontrolle auf Strukturbildung in subexzitatorischen Netzen untersucht. Ohne Rückkopplung sterben in subexzitatorischen Netzen alle Anregungswellen aus. Geeignete Rückkopplung bewirkt, dass Wellenfronten wachsen und sich die Anregungswellen über das gesamte Netz ausbreiten. Das heißt, zeitverzögerte Rückkopplungskontrolle kann die Ausbildung von Strukturen unterstützen oder erst möglich machen. In Netzen aus FitzHugh-Nagumo Elementen wird dieser Effekt im Detail für Wellenfronten studiert, die durch spezielle Startwerte, durch Rauschen oder durch Variabilität induziert werden. Für Wellen, die durch spezielle Startwerte oder durch Rauschen induziert werden, wird deren Ausbreitung im Netz für einen großen, zusammenhängenden Bereich an Verzögerungszeiten unterstützt. Die durch Rauschen induzierten Strukturen sind für mittlere Verzögerungszeiten am kohärentesten. Die Kohärenz der Strukturen und die damit verbundene Menge an übermittelter Information (Anzahl der Wellenfronten) zeigen eine resonanzartige Abhängigkeit von der Verzögerungszeit. Für durch Variabilität induzierte Wellenfronten ist die Netzdynamik noch komplexer. In gewissen Bereichen der Verzögerungszeit wird die Strukturbildung durch die Rückkopplung unterstützt, während in anderen jegliche Anregung unterdrückt wird. Mit Variabilität existieren oszillierende Elemente in dem subexzitatorischen Netz, von welchen sich die Wellenfronten ausbreiten. Da die Rückkopplungskontrolle aber für bestimmte Werte der Verzögerungszeit, den Fixpunkt einiger oszillierender Elemente stabilisiert, verharren in diesem Bereich der Verzögerungszeit alle Elemente im Fixpunkt, und es treten keine Strukturen auf. Auch hier wird die Abhängigkeit der Dynamik von der Anzahl der Elemente, die das Rückkopplungssignal bekommen, und von deren Korrelation untersucht. Es kann ausreichend sein, 40% aller Elemente per Rückkopplung zu kontrollieren, um zu erreichen, dass das Netz exzitatorisches Verhalten zeigt. Hierbei begünstigt eine starke Korrelation der kontrollierten Elemente die Ausbildung von kohärenten Strukturen. Die Ergebnisse bezüglich der Ausbreitung von Wellenfronten, welche durch spezielle Startbedingungen induziert werden, bestätigen sich auch für Netze aus Hodgkin-Huxley-Elementen.

Die Ergebnisse belegen, dass geeignete Rückkopplungskontrolle einen massiven Einfluss auf Strukturbildungsprozesse hat. Vor allem das Zusammenspiel von Rauschen und Rückkopplung, welches bei mittleren Verzögerungszeiten zu maximaler Kohärenz der Strukturen und maximalem Informationsübertrag führt, dürfte interessante Anwendungen in Systemen haben, in denen Informationstransport wichtig ist.

In Kapitel 7 wird der Einfluss von Rauschen und Variabilität auf Netze aus bistabilen FitzHugh-Nagumo-Elementen untersucht. Es wird gezeigt, dass sowohl multiplikatives Rauschen als auch multiplikative Variabilität einen systematischen Einfluss auf die Netzdynamik haben. Ausgehend vom asymmetrischen bistabilen Verhalten (die Schwelle für einen Übergang von einem stabilen Fixpunkt zum anderen und die Schwelle für den umgekehrten Übergang sind ungleich) wird durch Rauschen oder Variabilität symmetrisches bistabiles Verhalten induziert (gleiche Schwellen für die Übergänge). Diese Änderung in der Netzdynamik wird durch die theoretischen Näherungen, die in Kapitel 4 eingeführt wurden,

93

gut beschrieben. Vor allem die sogenannte Small Noise Expansion liefert eine genaue Vorhersage der Netzdynamik. Des Weiteren wird in Kapitel 7 das Antwortverhalten des Netzes auf ein schwaches externes Signal untersucht. Zunächst wird ausgehend vom symmetrischen bistabilen Regime der Einfluss von additivem Rauschen und additiver Variabilität auf das Antwortverhalten bestimmt. Bezüglich additiven Rauschens zeigt die Netzdynamik den bekannten Effekt der stochastischen Resonanz. Auch bezüglich der additiven Variabilität zeigt das Netz ein resonanzartiges Antwortverhalten (variability-induced resonance). Je stärker das Rauschen ist, desto weniger Variabilität ist nötig, um die Resonanz zu erreichen, und umgekehrt.

Danach erfolgt ausgehend vom asymmetrischen bistabilen Regime die Untersuchung des Einflusses additiver und multiplikativer Variabilität auf das Antwortverhalten. Es wird gezeigt, dass die Verstärkung des externen Signals in der Anwort des Netzes für mittlere Variabilitätsstärken von additiver und multiplikativer Variabilität (doubly variability-induced resonance) optimal ist. Die additive Variabilität induziert zwischen den beiden stabilen Fixpunkten Sprünge, die in Phase mit dem externen Signal sind, und die multiplikative Variabilität induziert das symmetrische bistabile Verhalten, für welches die Systemantwort maximal ist. Dieses Ergebnis gilt sowohl für global als auch für diffusiv gekoppelte Netze. Zuletzt wird schließlich noch der Einfluss von zeitverzögerter Rückkopplungskontrolle auf den Effekt der stochastischen Resonanz für ein einzelnes bistabiles Element und Netze aus bistabilen Elementen untersucht. Es wird gezeigt, dass die Verstärkung des externen Signals in der Systemantwort durch geeignete Rückkopplung nochmals erhöht werden kann.

Alle Ergebnisse zeigen, dass Rauschen, Variabilität und zeitverzögerte Rückkopplungskontrolle die Dynamik von räumlich ausgedehnten Systemen entscheidend beeinflussen und grundlegend ändern können. Vor allem die Ergebnisse für exzitatorische und oszillierende Netze könnten im Hinblick auf neuronale Krankheiten interessante Anwendungen finden. Zum Beispiel spielt die Unterdrückung von Oszillationen eine wichtige Rolle für neuronale Krankheiten (Parkinson, Epilepsie), bei denen synchrone Oszillationen von Nerven im Gehirn motorische Störungen bedingen. Bei Migräneanfällen spielt die Ausbreitung von Anregungswellen eine entscheidende Rolle. Die präsentierten Ergebnisse tragen hoffentlich dazu bei, neue Strategien zu entwickeln, um neurologische Störungen im Gehirn zu unterdrücken.

Bibliography

[1] M. C. Cross and P. C. Hohenberg. Pattern formation outside of equilibrium. *Rev. Mod. Phys.*, 65:851–1112, 1993.

[2] A. N. Zaikin and A. M. Zhabotinsky. Concentration wave propagation in two-dimensional liquid-phase self-oscillating system. *Nature*, 225:535–537, 1970.

[3] A. Gierer and H. Meinhardt. A theory of biological pattern formation. *Kybernetic*, 12:30–39, 1972.

[4] S. Sawai, P. A. Thomason, and E. C. Cox. An autoregulatory circuit for long-range self-organization in dictyostelium cell populations. *Nature*, 433:323–326, 2004.

[5] A. M. Turing. The chemical basis of morphogenesis. *Phil. Trans. R. Soc.*, 237:37–72, 1952.

[6] J. Hasty, J. Pradines, M. Dolnik, and J. J. Collins. Noise-based switches and amplifiers for gene expression. *PNAS*, 97:2075–2080, 2000.

[7] D. F. Russell, L. A. Wilkens, and F. Moss. Use of behavioural stochastic resonance by paddle fish for feeding. *Nature*, 402:291, 1999.

[8] A. Priplata, J. Niemi, M. Salen, J. Harry, L. A. Lipsitz, and J. J. Collins. Noise-enhanced human balance control. *Phys. Rev. Lett.*, 89:238101, 2002.

[9] C. van den Broeck, J. M. R. Parrondo, and R. Toral. Noise-induced nonequilibrium phase transition. *Phys. Rev. Lett.*, 73:3395, 1994.

[10] J. García-Ojalvo and J. M. Sancho. *Noise in Spatially Extended Systems*, Springer, Berlin, 1999.

[11] E. Ullner. *Noise-induced phenomena of signal transmission in excitable neural models*. Dissertation, Universität Potsdam, 2004.

[12] J. F. Lindner, S. Chandramouli, A. R. Bulsara, M. Löcher, and W. L. Ditto. Noise enhanced propagation. *Phys. Rev. Lett.*, 81:5048–5051, 1998.

[13] F. Sagues, J. M. Sancho, and J. García-Ojalvo. Spatiotemporal order out of noise. *Rev. Mod. Phys.*, 79:829, 2007.

[14] L. Gammaitoni, P. Hänggi, P. Jung, and F. Marchesoni. Stochastic resonance. *Rev. Mod. Phys.*, 70:223, 1998.

[15] F. Moss, A. Bulsara, and M. F. Shlesinger. Stochastic resonance in physics and biology. *J. Stat. Phys.*, 70, 1993.

[16] C. T. Haas, S. Turbanski, K. Kessler, and D. Schmidtbleicher. The effects of random whole-body-vibration on motor symptoms in Parkinson's disease. *NeuroRehabilitation*, 21:29–36, 2006.

[17] E. Glatt, M. Gassel, and F. Kaiser. Variability-sustained pattern formation in subexcitable media. *Phys. Rev. E*, 75:026206, 2007.

[18] M.-T. Hütt, H. Busch, and F. Kaiser. The effect of biological variability on spatiotemporal patterns - model simulations for a network of biochemical oscillators. *Nova Acta Leopoldina NF 88*, 332:381, 2003.

[19] E. Glatt. *Pattern Formation in Spatially Extended Systems: Interplay of Noise and Variability*. Dissertation, TU Darmstadt, 2008.

[20] E. Glatt, M. Gassel, and F. Kaiser. Noise-induced synchronisation in heterogeneous nets of neural elements. *Europhys. Lett.*, 81:40004, 2008.

[21] C. J. Tessone, C. R. Mirasso, R. Toral, and J. D. Gunton. Diversity-induced resonance. *Phys. Rev. Lett.*, 97:194101, 2006.

[22] R. Toral, C. J. Tessone, and J. V. Lopes. Collective effects induced by diversity in extended systems. *European Physical Journal - Special Topics*, 143:59, 2007.

[23] M. Gassel, E. Glatt, and F. Kaiser. Doubly variability-induced resonance. *Phys. Rev. E*, 76:016203, 2007.

[24] K. Pyragas. Continuous control of chaos by self-controlling feedback. *Physics Letters A*, 170:421–428, 1992.

[25] M. Dahlem, F. Schneider, and E. Schöll. Failure of feedback as a putative common mechanism of spreading depolarizations in migraine and stroke. *Chaos*, 18:026110, 2008.

[26] P. A. Tass. Effective desynchronization with bipolar double-pulse stimulation. *Phys. Rev. E*, 66:036226, 2002.

[27] M. G. Rosenblum and A. S. Pikovsky. Controlling synchronization in an ensemble of globally coupled oscillators. *Phys. Rev. Lett.*, 92:114102, 2004.

[28] O. V. Popovych, C. Hauptmann, and P. A. Tass. Effective desynchronization by nonlinear delayed feedback. *Phys. Rev. Lett.*, 94:164102, 2005.

[29] M. Gassel, E. Glatt, and F. Kaiser. Time-delayed feedback in a net of neural elements: Transition from oscillatory to excitable dynamics. *Fluctuation and Noise Letters*, 7:225–229, 2007.

[30] K. Pyragas, O. V. Popovych, and P. A. Tass. Controlling synchrony in oscillatory networks with a separate stimulation-registration setup. *Euro. Phys. Lett.*, 80:40002, 2007.

[31] A. Pikovsky and J. Kurths. Coherence resonance in a noise-driven excitable system. *Phys. Rev. Lett.*, 78:775, 1997.

[32] P. Jung and G. Mayer-Kress. Spatiotemporal stochastic resonance in excitable media. *Phys. Rev. Lett.*, 74:2130–2133, 1995.

[33] H. Busch and F. Kaiser. Influence of spatiotemporally correlated noise on structure formation in excitable media. *Phys. Rev. E*, 67:041105, 2003.

[34] B. Hauschildt, N.B. Janson, A. Balanov, and E. Schöll. Noise-induced cooperative dynamics and its control in coupled neuron models. *Phys. Rev. E.*, 74:051906, 2006.

[35] A. T. Winfree. Biological rhythms and the behavior of populations of coupled oscillators. *J. Theor. Biol.*, 16:15–42, 1967.

[36] Y. Kuramoto. Chemical oscillations, waves and turbulence. 1984.

[37] J. S. Nagumo and S. Yoshizawa. An active pulse transmission line simulating nerve axon. *Proc. Inst. Radio Engineers*, 50:2061, 1962.

[38] E. Glatt, M. Gassel, and F. Kaiser. Variability induced transition in a net of neural elements: From oscillatory to excitable behavior. *Phys. Rev. E*, 73:066230, 2006.

[39] M. Gassel. *Einfluss von Rauschen und biologischer Variabilität auf ein Netz aus FitzHugh-Nagumo-Elementen.* Diplomarbeit, TU Darmstadt, 2005.

[40] O. Föllinger. *Regelungstechnik, Einführung in die Methoden und ihre Anwendung.* Hüthig Verlag, Heidelberg, 1994.

[41] M. Münkel, F. Kaiser, and O. Hess. Spatiotemporal dynamics in multistripe semiconductor lasers with delayed optical feedback. *Phys. Lett. A*, 222:67–75, 1996.

[42] I. Fischer, O. Hess, W. Elsäßer, and E. Göbel. Complex spatio-temporal dynamics in the near-field of a broad-area semiconductor laser. *Europhys. Lett.*, 35:579–584, 1996.

[43] M. Münkel, F. Kaiser, and O. Hess. Stabilization of spatiotemporally chaotic semiconductor laser arrays by means of delayed optical feedback. *Phys. Rev. E*, 56:3868–3875, 1997.

[44] D. Goldobin, M. Rosenblum, and A. Pikovsky. Controlling oscillator coherence by delayed feedback. *Phys. Rev. E*, 67:061119, 2003.

[45] N.B. Janson, A.G. Balanov, and E. Schöll. Delayed feedback as a mean of control of noise-induced motion. *Phys. Rev. Lett.*, 93:010601, 2004.

[46] P. Hövel, M. Dahlem, and E. Schöll. Synchronization of noise-induced oscillations by time-delayed feedback. *Proc. 19th Internat. Conf. on Noise and Fluctuations*, 2007.

[47] P. Hövel and E. Schöll. Control of unstable steady states by time-delayed feedback methods. *Phys. Rev. E*, 72:046203, 2005.

[48] M. Gassel, E. Glatt, and F. Kaiser. Suppression of global oscillations via time-delayed feedback in a net of neural elements. *Proceedings of SPIE*, 6602:660213, 2007.

[49] O. Brandman and T. Meyer. Feedback loops shape cellular signals in space and time. *Science*, 322:390–395, 2008.

[50] H. Busch. Pattern formation and synchronization in excitable systems under the influence of spatiotemporal colored noise. *Dissertation*, Darmstadt, 2004.

[51] E. Glatt, H. Busch, A. Zaikin, and F. Kaiser. Noise-memory induced excitability and pattern formation in oscillatory neural models. *Phys. Rev. E*, 73:026216, 2006.

[52] A. L. Hodgkin and A. F. Huxley. A quantitative description of membrane current and its application to conduction and excitation in nerve. *J. Physiol.*, 117:500–544, 1952.

[53] P. Bak, K. Chen, and C. Tang. A forest-fire model and some thoughts on turbulence. *Phys. Lett. A*, 147:297, 1990.

[54] B. Drossel and F. Schwabl. Self-organized critical forest-fire model. *Phys. Rev. Lett.*, 69:1629–1632, 1992.

[55] S. Alonso, I. Sendina-Nadal, V. Perez-Munuzuri, J. M. Sancho, and F. Sagues. Regular wave propagation out of noise in chemical activ media. *Phys. Rev. Lett.*, 69:1629–1632, 1992.

[56] H. Beug, F. E. Katz, and G. Gerisch. Dictyostelium discoideum. *J. Cell Biol.*, 56:647–658, 1973.

[57] K. F. Bonhoeffer. Activation of passive iron as a model for the excitation of nerve. *J. Gen. Physiol.*, 32:69–91, 1948.

[58] R. A. FitzHugh. Impulse and physiological states in theoretical models of nerve membranes. *Biophys. J.*, 1:445, 1961.

[59] J. Keener and J. Snyder. *Mathematical Physiology*, Springer, New York, 1998.

[60] J. Moehlis. Canards for a reduction of the hodgkin-huxley equations. *Springer*, 225:535–537, 2005.

[61] J. M. Sancho, M. S. Miguel, S. L. Katz, and J. D. Gunton. Analytical and numerical studies of multiplicative noise. *Phys. Rev. A*, 26:1589–1609, 1981.

[62] E. Glatt. *Einfluss von multiplikativem Rauschen auf das FitzHugh-Nagumo-System*. Diplomarbeit, TU Darmstadt, 2004.

[63] E. A. Novikov. Functionals and the random force method in turbulence theory. *Sov. Phys.*, 20:1920–1926, 1964.

[64] N. G. van Kampen. *Stochastic Processes in Physics and Chemistry*. North Holland, Amsterdam, 2001.

[65] S. De Monte, F. d´Ovidio, and E. Mosekilde. Coherent regimes of globally coupled dynamical systems. *Phys. Rev. Lett.*, 90:054102, 2003.

[66] I. Gomes Da Silva, S. De Monte, F. d´Ovidio, R. Toral, and C. R. Mirasso. Coherent regimes of mutually coupled chua´s circuits. *Phys. Rev. E*, 73:036203, 2006.

[67] M.-Th. Hütt, R. Neff, H. Busch, and F. Kaiser. Method for detecting the signature of noise-induced structures in spatiotemporal data sets. *Phys. Rev. E*, 66:026117, 2002.

[68] S. Yamada, M. Nakashima, K. Matsumoto, and S. Shiono. Information theoretic analysis of action potential trains: I. analysis of correlation between two neurons. *Biol. Cybern.*, 68:215–220, 1993.

[69] S. Yamada, M. Nakashima, K. Matsumoto, and S. Shiono. Information theoretic analysis of action potential trains: Ii. analysis of correlation among n neurons to deduce connection structure. *J. Neurosci. Methods*, 66:35–45, 1996.

[70] E. Ullner, A. Zaikin, J. García-Ojalvo, and J. Kurths. Noise-induced excitability in oscillatory media. *Phys. Rev. Lett.*, 91:180601, 2003.

[71] D. V. Ramana Reddy, A. Sen, and G. L. Johnston. Time delay induced death in coupled limit cycle oscillators. *Phys. Rev. Lett.*, 80:5109–5112, 1998.

[72] D. G. Aronson, G. B. Ermentrout, and N. Kopell. Amplitude response of coupled oscillators. *Physica D*, 41:403, 1990.

[73] P. Jung, A. Cornell-Bell, F. Moss, S. Kadar, J. Wang, and K. Showalter. Noise sustained waves in subexcitable media: from chemical waves to brain waves. *Chaos*, 8:567, 1998.

[74] S. Alonso, F. Sagues, and J. M. Sancho. Excitability transitions and wave dynamics under spatiotemporal structured noise. *Phys. Rev. E*, 65:066107, 2002.

[75] S. K. Aurora, B. K. Ahmad, K. M. A. Welch, P. Bhardhwaj, and N. M. Ramadan. Transcranial magnetic stimulation confirms hyperexcitability of occipital cortex in migraine. *Neurology*, 50:1111–1114, 1998.

[76] M. A. Dahlem and S. C. Müller. Reaction-diffusion waves in neuronal tissue and the window of cortical excitability. *Ann. Phys.*, 13:442 – 449, 2004.

[77] M. A. Dahlem and E. P. Chronicle. A computational perspective on migraine aura. *Progress in Neurobiology*, 74:351 – 361, 2004.

[78] J. Schlesner, V. Zykov, H. Engel, and E. Schöll. Stabilization of unstable rigid rotation of spiral waves in excitable media. *Phys. Rev. E*, 74:046215, 2006.

[79] M. Gassel, E. Glatt, and F. Kaiser. Delay-sustained pattern formation in subexcitable media. *Phys. Rev. E*, 77:066220, 2008.

[80] C. Zhou, J. Kurths, and B. Hu. Array-enhanced coherence resonance: Nontrivial effects of heterogeneity and spatial independence of noise. *Phys. Rev. Lett.*, 87:098101, 2001.

[81] B. Lindner, J. García-Ojalvo, A. Neiman, and L. Schimansky-Geier. Effects of noise in excitable systems. *Phys. Rep.*, 392:321, 2004.

[82] A. Zaikin, J. Kurths, and L. Schimansky-Geier. Doubly stochastic resonance. *Phys. Rev. Lett.*, 85:227, 2003.

[83] A. Zaikin, J. García-Ojalvo, R. Bascones, E. Ullner, and J. Kurths. Doubly stochastic coherence via noise-induced symmetry in bistable neural models. *Phys. Rev. Lett.*, 90:030601, 2003.

[84] W. H. Eccles and F. W. Jordan. A trigger relay utilizing three-electrode thermionic vacuum tubes. *The Electrician*, 83:298, 1919.

[85] F. Schlögl. Chemical reaction models for nonequilibrium phase-transitions. *Z. Physik*, 253:147, 1972.

[86] L.S. Tsimring and A. Pikovsky. Noise-induced dynamics in bistable systems with delay. *Phys. Rev. Lett.*, 87:250602, 2001.

[87] T. Prager, H.-P. Lerch, L. Schimansky-Geier, and E. Schöll. Increase of coherence in excitable systems by delayed feedback. *J. Phys. A: Math. Theor.*, 40:11045–11055, 2007.

[88] S. Kim, S. H. Park, and H.-B. Pyo. Stochastic resonance in coupled oscillator systems with time delay. *Phys. Rev. Lett.*, 82:1620, 1999.

Danksagung

Ich möchte an dieser Stelle noch denjenigen Personen meinen Dank aussprechen, ohne deren Unterstützung diese Arbeit sicher nicht in ihrer heutigen Form vorliegen würde.

Zuerst möchte ich *Herrn Prof. Friedemann Kaiser* dafür danken, dass er mir die Promotion in seiner Arbeitsgruppe ermöglicht und stets für ein sehr angenehmes Arbeitsverhältnis gesorgt hat. Von seiner umfassenden Erfahrung auf dem Gebiet der nichtlinearen Dynamik, seinen Ideen und Anregungen, und den Diskussionen in der Arbeitsgruppe habe ich sehr profitiert. Außerdem konnte ich in relativ kurzer Zeit Einblick in viele Bereiche des "wissenschaftlichen Alltags" bekommen.

Meinen beiden Kollegen *Erik Glatt* und *Tobias Richter* gilt mein besonderer Dank für die entspannte und freundschaftliche Zusammenarbeit. Mit ihnen konnte ich jederzeit Ideen und Forschungsergebnisse diskutieren, und darüber hinaus bei Computer- und Programmierproblemen ihren Rat einholen. Besonders danke ich *Erik Glatt* für die direkte wissenschaftliche Zusammenarbeit.

Prof. Eckehard Schöll und seiner Arbeitsgruppe an der Technischen Universität Berlin danke ich für die Einladung zu einem Kolloquiumsvortrag und die darauf folgenden äußerst produktiven Diskussionen. Vor allem gilt mein Dank *Dr. Markus Dahlem* für neue Ideen, lange Diskussionen und einen Einblick in mögliche medizinische Anwendungen in der Migräneforschung.

Des Weiteren möchte ich mich bei *Prof. Felicitas Pfeifer*, *Monika Medina* und wiederum bei *Erik Glatt* bedanken, dass ich als Kollegiat des Graduiertenkollegs 340 der Technischen Universität Darmstadt an Workshops des Graduiertenkollegs teilnehmen durfte und somit einen guten Einblick in biologische und biophysikalische Prozesse bekam.

Mein ganz besonderer Dank gebührt meinen Eltern, die mich jederzeit auf vielfältige Weise unterstützt und gefördert haben.

Abschließend möchte ich mich bei meiner Familie, meinen Freunden und vor allem bei meiner Freundin *Linda Stenzel* für Abwechslung, Kurzweil, Unterhaltung und Motivation während der Zeit der Promotion bedanken.

Die VDM Verlagsservicegesellschaft sucht für wissenschaftliche Verlage abgeschlossene und herausragende

Dissertationen, Habilitationen, Diplomarbeiten, Master Theses, Magisterarbeiten usw.

für die kostenlose Publikation als Fachbuch.

Sie verfügen über eine Arbeit, die hohen inhaltlichen und formalen Ansprüchen genügt, und haben Interesse an einer honorarvergüteten Publikation?

Dann senden Sie bitte erste Informationen über sich und Ihre Arbeit per Email an *info@vdm-vsg.de*.

Sie erhalten kurzfristig unser Feedback!

VDM Verlagsservicegesellschaft mbH
Dudweiler Landstr. 99   Telefon +49 681 3720 174
D - 66123 Saarbrücken   Fax   +49 681 3720 1749
www.vdm-vsg.de

Die VDM Verlagsservicegesellschaft mbH vertritt

Printed by Books on Demand GmbH, Norderstedt / Germany